D0521861

Irish Country House Cooking

Irish Country House Cooking

The Blue Book Recipe Collection

Georgina Campbell

Photographs by Rai Uhlemann

EPICURE PRESS

Published 2005 by
EPICURE PRESS
P.O. Box 6173, Dublin 13.

Text copyright Georgina Campbell 2005
Photographs joint copyright Rai Uhlemann/Blue Book 2005

ISBN 1-903164-13-3

ACKNOWLEDGMENTS

Many thanks to Hilary Finlay and all the members of Ireland's Blue Book and their hard-working staffs, for making this book possible. Thanks also to Brian Darling at The Design Station for his work on design, and to our photographer, Rai Uhlemann for conveying a unique sense of the food in these wonderful establishments.

On a personal note I must once again thank my husband, William, a great travelling companion for whom no detour is too much trouble (especially if, as is so often the case in Ireland, it involves exploring a little known piece of coastline, or visiting a remote harbour).

Lastly, I also owe a great debt of gratitude to my late parents, Brian and Jean Campbell, for the invaluable gifts of an appreciation of good food and country life. They loved the many Blue Book houses they visited with me over the years and this book is gratefully dedicated to their memory.

Georgina Campbell.

Design: Brian Darling, The Design Station, Dublin.
Photography: Rai Uhlemann
               Additional photography courtesy of Ireland's Blue Book and WM Nixon.

Printed and bound in Italy.

PHOTOGRAPHY:
Cover -   Restaurant Patrick Guilbaud;
                   L'Ecrivain; Glin Castle; Dunbrody House
Back Cover -   Currarevagh House
Front Flap -   Stella Maris Hotel
Title pages -   Ballymaloe Cookery School; Castle Durrow;
Contents Page - The Mustard Seed at Echo Lodge; Dunbrody House; Longueville House; Enniscoe House
Introduction -   Chapter One; Newport House; Currarevagh House

Contents

Introduction

Welcome to the fourth edition of Irish Country House Cooking, a book that illustrates the diverse styles of hospitality offered by Ireland's longest established and most quality-conscious association of country houses and restaurants. From the outset, The Blue Book - originally named the Irish Country Houses & Restaurants Association when it was formed in 1974 - established standards of excellence which have stood by the organisation ever since, as stringent membership rules ensured that only the most committed establishments would join. The idea certainly appealed to hosts who were in for the long haul, as demonstrated by the fact that six of the original 17 are still members: Ballymaloe House and Longueville House in County Cork, Cashel House and Currarevagh House in Connemara, Caragh Lodge in Kerry, and Hunter's Hotel in County Wicklow are all not only active, but have a new generation coming up who are now equally inspirational in their leadership.

Visitors to Irish country houses have always loved the simple pleasures like home-made brown bread, the open fires burning logs or turf, the feeling of being a guest in someone's lovely old house - and, above all, finding that their hosts have time to talk to them about its history and places of interest to visit in their area, not to mention other country houses of their acquaintance and the most scenic routes to take to reach them. And, while the houses themselves are generally of architectural interest, the main historical interest is often in the owners themselves, many of them from families who have lived in these properties for hundreds of years - something which has a special fascination for guests who are making a temporary escape from the hurly burly of today's hectic world and find this way of life, with not only properties but now also businesses passed on from generation to generation, very reassuring.

Providing guests with the very best food available has always been a special feature of Blue Book hospitality so it is appropriate that, while the houses are rural - set in their own grounds and preferably of historic architecture - membership rules for restaurants have always been more relaxed, and restaurants in coastal towns like Dingle, Youghal and Howth have been members for many years. More recently, the arrival of three of Dublin's top restaurants as new members has introduced an exciting cosmopolitan atmosphere to this group of dedicated chefs and cooks.

Food as fashion was a long way off when the original group got together in the 1970s, but an understanding of true hospitality and a fundamental respect for quality ingredients are qualities shared by all the houses and restaurants, whether low key country houses or smart city restaurants. Long before it was fashionable, food in Irish country houses was what is now known as ingredients led - their kitchens were supplied by their walled gardens, their own estates and rivers and, of course, the sea, which is never far away from any kitchen in Ireland and accounts for the enormous popularity of seafood throughout the country. Superb raw ingredients have always been the basis of true country house cooking and, today, the best city restaurants follow the same pattern, seeking the very best fresh and specialist produce from the same, or very similar, sources.

So this book is much more than a collection of recipes: from the homely to the very grand, it celebrates the diversity of Irish country houses and their food, and also some very special restaurants. The dishes selected vary greatly in style, as the establishments themselves do, and all are clearly explained for home cooks to recreate with confidence.

For those who have visited any of the houses or restaurants represented here, I hope this book will bring back happy memories for you as it certainly has done for me while we have been working on it. In the introduction to each property I have tried to encapsulate what seems to me to be the essence of the place although, I am sure, Rai Uhlemann's evocative photography will do the job far better. Whether or not you are familiar with the houses, they say something important about Ireland, her history, her hospitality and, of course, her food. As to the recipes, they have been selected to give an accurate reflection of the food of each house, but also with a particular emphasis on accessibility for home cooks. In other words, far from being just 'restaurant dishes', this is real food - so I hope you will enjoy it with your families and friends.

Georgina Campbell.

Georgina Campbell,
Editor.

Aherne's seafood bar & restaurant

Youghal, Co Cork

Youghal is perhaps most famous for its association with Sir Walter Raleigh, or its location at the mouth of one of Ireland's most renowned fishing rivers, the beautiful Blackwater - but, today, the main attraction for many visitors to this historic walled port is a call at Aherne's. Currently in its third generation of family ownership, this impressive establishment offers luxurious accommodation and warm hospitality, but it is for their food - and, especially, the ultra-fresh seafood which comes straight from the fishing boats in Youghal harbour - that Aherne's is especially renowned. While John FitzGibbon supervises the front of house - and somehow always manages to be in three places at once as they have two bars as well as the restaurant - his brother David reigns over a busy kitchen catering for food served in both bars, as well as evening meals in the restaurant. The bar menu is extensive and admirably simple in style - oysters, chowder, smoked salmon (all served with their renowned moist dark brown yeast bread) are all typical.

Hot shellfish with garlic, herbs, olive oil & white wine

This exuberant mélange of fresh shellfish is a speciality, and is simple to make if you have access to the ingredients. It would make a dramatic centrepiece for party, and quantities are flexible.

Serves about 8
8 crab claws
12-16 whole prawns
8 rock oysters
24 shrimps
24 mussels
1 bottle of white wine
4 cloves of garlic
4 tbsp / 5 US tablespoons olive oil
1 lobster, freshly cooked (optional)
Freshly chopped herbs: chives,
    parsley, basil and coriander

In a large pan, place the crab claws, prawns, oysters, shrimps, mussels, white wine, garlic and olive oil. Cook over fairly high heat for about 8-10 minutes, or until the mussels and oysters open.

Tumble everything together in a large bowl, adding in the warm lobster meat and claws if using. Sprinkle the fresh herbs over the succulent shellfish, and serve with plenty of crusty white bread.

Cod with a parmesan & chive butter crust

Aherne's is renowned for the quality of the seafood served, which is landed at the harbour in Youghal and other nearby fishing ports. This is a simple dish for the home cook to make, and David likes to serve it with a provençal style fresh tomato sauce.

Serves 4
2oz / 50g / ⅓ cup parmesan cheese, cubed
2oz / 50g / 1 cup chives, chopped
3oz / 75g / ¾ stick butter, cubed
2oz / 50g / 1 cup breadcrumbs
salt and pepper
4 x 7 oz / 200g fillets of cod

Place the parmesan cheese in a food processor, and process until the cheese is finely chopped, then add the chives and process again briefly to mix. Add the butter and breadcrumbs, then season to taste with salt and pepper. Refrigerate for 1-2 hours until quite firm - like a green-speckled butter.

When ready to cook, preheat a hot oven 400°F / 200°C / gas mark 6.

Pat the cod fillets dry with kitchen paper, then spread the mixture evenly over each one and place in a greased baking tin. Bake in the preheated oven for about 10 minutes, or until the fish is just cooked through - this will depend on the thickness of the fillets, which will be opaque when cooked, and flake when tested with a fork.

Serve with fresh seasonal vegetables.

Eileen's shortbread biscuits

These tried and trusted biscuits are really good with coffee, or the famous Barry's Tea, from Cork city.

Makes about 2 dozen

4 oz / 110g / ½ cup caster sugar
4 oz / 110g / 1 stick butter, softened
4 oz / 110g / 8 US tablespoons margarine, soft
12 oz / 350g / 3 cups plain white flour

Using your fingers, blend the caster sugar, butter, margarine and flour until they bind together to form a stiff dough. Place in the fridge to rest for one hour.

Preheat a fairly hot oven, 375°F / 190°C / gas mark 5.

Roll out the dough gently to about ⅓ inch / 1 cm thick, shaping the edges neatly with your fingers as you work. Using a biscuit cutter, cut the dough into rounds, then prick with a fork to prevent the biscuits rising in the oven. Lay out on lightly greased baking sheets and bake for about 8 minutes, or until golden brown. Cool on a wire rack and store in an airtight container until required.

Ardtara

Upperlands, Co Londonderry

Former home to the Clark linen milling family, Ardtara is now an elegantly decorated Victorian country house of great charm, with fine high-ceilinged rooms, antique furnishings, fresh flowers everywhere - and a welcoming atmosphere. Large, luxuriously furnished bedrooms overlook the garden and surrounding woodland walks, and the old snooker room is converted from its previous use to make a unique dining room – still with full Victorian skylight and original hunting frieze. Good food is at the heart of this hospitable house and it is the philosophy to use seasonal and local ingredients, including game in season and local meats supplied by McKees of Maghera, who are members of the Elite Guild of Butchers. Irish farmhouse cheeses are served with the famous Dittys oat biscuits, which are made locally.

Sticky toffee and ginger pudding with toffee sauce

Traditional puddings are appealing in the colder months, and this is a good winter dinner party dessert, as it can be made the day before and warmed up when needed.

Serves 10-12
9 oz / 250g block of dried dates
3/4 pt / 450ml / 2 cups water
1 1/2 tsp bicarbonate of soda
3 oz / 75g / 3/4 stick soft butter
9 oz / 250g / 1 cup soft brown sugar
9 oz / 250g / 2 cups plain flour
3 egg, lightly beaten
1 oz / 30g / 1/4 cup stem ginger, finely
  chopped

Sauce:
9 oz / 250g / 1 cup caster sugar
1 pint / 600ml / 2 1/4 whipping cream

Preheat a cool oven, 150°C / 300°F / gas mark 2. Put the chopped dates into a pan with the water and warm until they have softened. Allow to cool, then add the bicarbonate of soda and blend lightly with a hand blender. Cream the butter and sugar together in a mixer for about 5 minutes, or beat with a wooden spoon until light and fluffy. Cream well, scraping down the sides of the bowl frequently to ensure the mixture is thoroughly blended. Mix in the eggs and flour a little at a time, then finally add the chopped ginger and the date mixture. Pour the mixture into a deep sided baking tin lined with greaseproof paper and bake in the preheated oven for 45 minutes, or until a knife comes out clean when placed in the middle. Allow to cool.

To make the sauce: Just cover the bottom of a heavy based pan with water, and place over moderate heat. Slowly pour in the sugar, allowing it to dissolve gradually. Do not shake pan, but allow the sugar to turn to a golden brown colour. Carefully pour in the cream (the sugar will spit at this stage), then slowly boil for 5 minutes, whisking every now and then. Allow to cool. When cold, cut the pudding into squares and store in a plastic container.

To serve: spoon some sauce over, cover with a lid and microwave until steaming hot. Serve with home-made, or good quality commercial, ice cream.

Spring roll of ham hock and fennel with caper jelly and mustard mayonnaise

This popular starter is a speciality at Ardtara, and guests enjoy the unexpected use of local ingredients.

Serves 8
2 ham hocks
For the stock:
1 stick celery, roughly chopped
1 white leek, trimmed, washed & roughly chopped
1 clove garlic, peeled & left whole
1 carrot, peeled & roughly chopped
1 small onion, peeled & roughly chopped
1 small bunch thyme, rosemary and bayleaf
To complete the dish:
2oz / 50g / 3 US tablespoons grain mustard
pinch of freshly chopped parsley
pinch of fennel seeds (lightly dry roasted)
1oz / 20g / 1 US tablespoon capers
2oz / 50g / 3 US tablespoons mayonnaise
pinch of freshly chopped chives
8 spring roll wrappers

To cook the ham: Put the ham hocks into a large pan and cover with cold water. Bring to a simmer over moderate heat, skimming off any scum that comes to the top. Add the vegetables and herbs, then bring back up to boiling point but do not allow to boil. Simmer very gently for 4 hours, or until the small bone in the ham hock comes out with ease. Allow the meat to cool in the cooking liquor.

To make the fillings: When the ham hocks are cold, remove them from the pan, reserving the cooking liquor; flake off the meat, discarding the skin and any fat, sinew or gristle. Mix the meat with half of the mustard, the parsley and the fennel seeds; moisten with a little of the ham stock, but take care not to make the mixture too wet. Adjust the seasoning with plenty of freshly ground pepper, and a little salt if necessary (the ham may be salty).

To make the caper jelly: Pass the cooking liquor through a fine strainer and measure off ⅓ pint / 200 ml (the rest will make useful stock for pea and ham soup); add the capers to the measured stock, and refrigerate overnight to make a jelly.

To make the mustard mayonnaise: Mix the mayonnaise with the remaining mustard and the chives, and set aside.

To complete: Following the instructions on the pack, fill the spring roll wrappers with the ham mixture to make eight spring rolls then, as they cook better when frozen, put them into the freezer and leave until solid.

To cook: Heat fresh oil to 350°F / 180°C in the deep fryer, then cook the spring rolls in batches until crisp, golden and heated through.

To serve: Cut the spring rolls at an angle and serve upright on large warm plates, with a crisp salad garnish and dipping dishes of the mustard mayonnaise and caper jelly.

Ballylickey Manor House

Bantry, Co Cork

Built some 300 years ago by Lord Kenmare, as a shooting lodge, Ballylickey Manor has now been the home of the Franco-Irish Graves family for four generations. It is perfectly poised on the boundary of Cork and Kerry in Ireland's magnificent south-western corner, and has many facets to its personality, each of interest to different kinds of guest. For some, there's the literary connection with the poet Robert Graves, who was an uncle of the present owner, George Graves, and visited the house on many occasions. Garden lovers, however, will especially appreciate the formal, park-like gardens, laid out along the river bank many years ago by George's mother, Kitty, creating a wonderful framework for sweeping views over Bantry Bay. The casual visitor, on the other hand, may admire the elegance of the main house, which has been restored and impressively furnished by George and Christiane Graves to match its period, or simply consider a spot of salmon or trout fishing on its own private stretch of river, or a little light exercise in the heated outdoor pool followed by a leisurely meal in the elegant period restaurant.

Apple and cinnamon chocolate mousse

Everyone loves a classic chocolate mousse and this Ballylickey version has a special twist.

Serves 4

*4 Cox's orange pippins or an
    alternative crisp eating apple
1 tablespoon / 1¹/₄ US tablespoons
    caster sugar
a pinch of ground cinnamon
1-2 tbsp / 1¹/₄ - 2¹/₂ US tablespoons
    unsalted butter
1-2 tbsp / 1¹/₄ - 2¹/₂ US tablespoons
    dark rum, or to taste*

For the mousse:

*9oz / 250g best dark chocolate
a little milk
3 eggs, separated
5 fl oz / 150ml / ³/₄ cup cream*

Peel and core the apples, and cut into cubes. Place on a plate and sprinkle with the sugar and cinnamon. Set aside for about half an hour. When ready to cook, heat a non-stick pan, melt the butter and lightly cook the apples until golden and sticky. Flambé with the dark rum and allow to cool.

To make the mousse: Break the chocolate into pieces and melt slowly in a bowl over a pan of barely simmering water, adding a little milk to prevent the chocolate from granulating. When smooth and warm, add the three egg yolks into the chocolate, mixing gently but thoroughly. Pour into a measuring jug or bowl and allow the mixture to cool completely. When cold add the whipped cream, which should be about one third of the volume of the chocolate mixture. Whisk the eggs whites until they are stiff, making about half of the volume of the chocolate mixture and, using a metal spoon, carefully fold into the chocolate cream mixture to make a smooth mousse.

To finish the dish: Chill in the fridge for 1 hour, then fold the prepared apples into the chocolate mixture. Turn into a glass serving bowl, or divide between four individual dishes, and refrigerate for four hours until set. Decorate in any way you like before serving.

Cod and spinach lasagne

Visitors to the south-west of Ireland especially enjoy the fresh seafood - and guests at Ballylickey Manor find this attractive dish easy to make at home.

Serves 4
2 lb / 900g fillets of cod
9oz / 250g / 4 cups baby spinach
1-2 tbsp / 1$\frac{1}{4}$ - 2$\frac{1}{2}$ US tablespoons olive oil
9oz / 250g lasagne
6-8 large tomatoes
1 clove garlic, peeled and finely chopped
a little grated parmesan (Irish farmhouse cheeses that may be used instead are Gabriel and Desmond, both made in Co Cork)

Preheat a hot oven, 400°F / 200°C / gas mark 6.

To prepare the filling: Poach or steam the cod fillets until just cooked. Over moderate heat, toss the baby spinach lightly in the olive oil until half cooked. Allow the cod and spinach to cool. Flake the cod with a fork.

To make a tomato coulis: Immerse the tomatoes briefly in boiling water to loosen the skins. Peel and de-seed them, remove the core and drain off any excess liquid. Chop finely or purée in a blender or food processor.

To complete: Cook the lasagne for 2 minutes (even if pre-cooked). Construct the lasagne in a buttered oven proof dish, starting with a layer of lasagne, then a layer of the tomato coulis, then the cod and finally the spinach. Proceed as above finishing with a layer of lasagne, tomato coulis and generous layer of grated parmesan. Finish with a little olive oil and a sprinkling of very finely chopped garlic. Bake in the preheated oven for around 35 minutes, until bubbling hot and nicely browned, then serve with a crisp green salad to accompany.

Ballymaloe House

Shanagarry, Co Cork

First time visitors to Ballymaloe are invariably charmed by the approach, through lush green fields with sheep grazing all around - the Allen family home may be Ireland's most famous country house, but they have always described it as 'a large family farmhouse'. And - although, with over thirty bedrooms, it is very large indeed - Ballymaloe remains true to that description over three decades after Myrtle and her husband, the late Ivan Allen, first welcomed guests to their home in 1964. The dining room - named The Yeats Room after their collection of Jack Yeats paintings - opened first, followed by rooms for accommodation in 1967, and family enterprises connected with Ballymaloe House now include not only the farmlands and gardens that supply the kitchen, but also a shop selling crafts, kitchenware and furniture, the Crawford Gallery Café in Cork city and Darina Allen's internationally acclaimed cookery school nearby. Yet Ballymaloe is still most remarkable for its unspoilt charm: although now rightly receiving international recognition for a lifetime's work "recapturing forgotten flavours, and preserving those that may soon die", Myrtle continues to supervise everything, ably assisted by her children and their families, and their teamwork is indeed a sight to behold.

Fresh orange jelly with mint

This is a fresh tasting little jelly which is made at Ballymaloe when the citrus fruit is at its best, just after Christmas. Blood oranges can be used and look wonderful. If mint is not available you could use lemon balm which seems to come up all year round in the gardens at Ballymaloe.

Serves 6-8
Jelly:
6 oranges
1 lemon
8 fl oz / 250ml / 1 1/2 cups syrup (made from 6 fl oz / 175ml / 3/4 cup water and 6oz / 170g / 3/4 cup sugar)
1 tsp Grand Marnier
2 rounded tsp gelatine
2 tbsp / 2 1/2 US tablespoons water
Sauce:
8 fl oz / 250ml / 1 cup fresh orange juice, sweetened to taste with caster sugar
2 tbsp / 3 US tablespoons chopped mint
Garnish:
Sprigs of mint or lemon balm

To make the jelly: Choose a terrine 1 1/2 lb / 900ml / 4 cups capacity, or 6-8 oval or round moulds 3 1/2 fl oz / 1/3 cup capacity. Line the terrine or moulds with cling film or brush with a tasteless oil. Grate the rind from two of the oranges very carefully, on a stainless steel grater (making sure you don't grate down to the pith). Segment all six oranges and add the syrup, orange zest, lemon juice and Grand Marnier. Mix well, then strain the liquid off the oranges and measure 1/2 pint / 300ml / 1 1/4 cup. Keep the remainder aside for the sauce. Soak the gelatine in two tablespoons of cold water in a small bowl for a few minute until it develops a sponge-like texture. Put the bowl into a saucepan of simmering water until the gelatine crystals have dissolved. Mix with the orange liquid, stirring carefully. Add the orange segments and fill into terrine or into 6-8 little oval or round moulds. Put in the fridge and allow to set for 3-4 hours .

For the sauce: Measure the remaining orange liquid and bring up to 8fl oz / 250ml / 1 cup with some more freshly squeezed orange juice. Taste and sweeten if necessary, add 2 tablespoons / 3 US tablespoons freshly chopped mint.

To serve: Unmould the jelly onto a serving dish or individual plates. Pour a little sauce around each jelly and garnish with mint leaves or variegated lemon balm.

Myrtle Allen: a lifetime's work "recapturing forgotten flavours, and preserving those that may soon die"

Braised and spiced lamb with lemon & coriander

At Ballymaloe it is traditional to wait until Easter to taste the first of the succulent new season lamb, and braising is a useful cooking method for slightly older animals. This unusual recipe combines whole and ground spices in the paste the meat is cooked in, and it is good served with a green vegetable such as spinach, purple sprouting broccoli or kale.

Serves 8-10

1 leg of lamb
1 tsp whole coriander seeds, toasted
¹/₂ tsp ground coriander
3 tsp whole cumin seed
1¹/₂ tsp ground cumin
2 tsp curry powder
sea salt & black pepper
1 tbsp / 1¹/₄ US tablespoons thyme
  leaves
1 dsp chopped rosemary
4 cloves garlic, peeled & finely
  chopped
15 fl oz / 435 ml / 2 cups chicken
  stock
2 tbsp / 2¹/₂ US tablespoons chopped
  coriander leaves
Lemon wedges to garnish.

Preheat a moderate oven, 350°F / 180°C / gas mark 4.

Combine all the herbs and spices, except the fresh coriander leaves, in a bowl. Heat the olive oil in a heavy based casserole and gently brown the meat all over. Discard the excess fat from the casserole. Season the meat with the sea salt and a grinding of black pepper, and cover with the herb and spice paste. Carefully pour the stock into the casserole, without dislodging the herb and spice topping on the lamb. Cover with a greaseproof paper lid, then the casserole lid, place in the preheated oven and cook for 90 minutes.

When the lamb is cooked, remove the casserole from the oven and put the lamb onto a serving dish to rest; keep warm. Remove the excess fat from the cooking liquor, and simmer over moderate heat to reduce to a richly flavoured gravy. Finally add the chopped coriander leaf to the gravy, and correct the seasoning. Carve the lamb and serve with the gravy, lemon wedges and the green vegetable of your choice.

Salad of Ardsallagh goats cheese with rocket leaves and Lisanley honey

This may seem like an unusual combination of ingredients but the result is a revelation, and the beauty here is the simplicity of the recipe. The delicious soft goats cheese used at Ballymaloe is from Carrigtowhill in County Cork, the rocket leaves are from their own garden and the honey comes from nearby Cloyne - whatever ingredients you choose to use, do source the very best quality.

Serves 4

4 handfuls of rocket leaves
2 soft Ardsallagh goats cheeses
  approx 2oz / 50g each
1 tbsp / 1¼ US tablespoons best
  quality honey
4 tbsp / 5 US tablespoons extra virgin
  olive oil
a pinch of Maldon salt
coarsely ground black pepper
squeeze of lemon juice

Divide the rocket leaves between 4 plates or 1 large, flat serving dish This is a flat salad so do not pile the leaves up. Just lay them in a single layer on the plates. Dice the goat's cheese into about ½ inch / 1cm dice, and sprinkle over the rocket leaves.

With the help of a teaspoon, drizzle the honey over the rocket and cheese in a grid pattern. Follow this with a drizzle of olive oil and a squeeze of lemon juice. Finally, season with a pinch of Maldon sea salt and a grinding of black pepper. Serve as soon as possible.

Ballymaloe Cookery School

Shanagarry, Co Cork

Darina Allen's internationally renowned Ballymaloe Cookery School is at Kinoith, just a couple of miles from Ballymaloe House. Here Darina introduces students to the best of produce from the area - notably fresh fish from nearby Ballycotton, and fresh fruit, vegetables and herbs from their own organic gardens, which are now almost as famous as the school itself. Hens pick around the gardens, providing a constant supply of free range eggs for the school, and their rare breed pigs are a reminder of the way pork used to taste, and much sought after by those in the know.

Rosemary and raisin soda bread

Soda bread takes only a few minutes to make. It's great to experiment with variations - try it with olives, sun dried tomatoes or caramelised onions added - the possibilities are endless. The amount of buttermilk given here works exactly with the Odlums Flour used at Ballymaloe Cookery School; however, other flours may absorb more or less liquid. Makes one round loaf.

1 lb / 450g / 4 cups, firmly packed plain white flour, preferably unbleached
1 level tsp salt
1 level tsp bread soda (bicarbonate of soda)
3oz / 75g / generous 1/2 cup raisins
2 tbsp fresh rosemary, chopped
Sour milk or buttermilk to mix - 14 fl oz / 400ml / 1 3/4 cups approx.

Soda bread must be baked as soon as it is mixed, so before you begin pre-heat a very hot oven to 450°F / 230°C / gas mark 8. Sieve the flour, salt and bread soda into a large bowl, then add the raisins and rosemary. Make a well in the centre. Pour all of the milk in at once. Using one hand, mix in the flour from the sides of the bowl, adding more milk if necessary. The dough should be soft, and not too wet and sticky. When it all comes together, turn it out onto a well floured work surface. Tidy up the shape and flip over gently. Pat the dough into a circle about 1½ inch / 4cm deep. It is traditional in Ireland to cut a cross on the top, to help the loaf to cook evenly. (Or, as Darina says, "To let the fairies out, so they won't jinx your bread"). Bake in the pre-heated oven for 15 minutes, then reduce the to temperature 400°F / 200°C / gas mark 6 and continue baking for a further 20-30 minutes, or until done. To test, tap the bottom of the bread: if it is fully cooked it will sound hollow.

Variation - Rosemary and Raisin Scones: Make the dough as above but flatten the dough into a circle about 1 inch / 2.5cm deep. Cut into scones. Scones take about 20 minutes to bake.

Summer fruit salad with sweet geranium leaves

Sweet geranium (Pelargonium Graveolens) and many other varieties of scented geraniums are on the windowsills at Ballymaloe Cookery School. The lemon scented leaves are used in all sorts of ways, and occasionally the pretty purple flowers also, to enliven and add magic to otherwise simple dishes. The crystallised leaves are wonderful with fresh cream cheese and juicy blackberries.

Serves 8-10
4oz / 110g / 1 cup raspberries
4oz / 110g / 1 cup loganberries
4oz / 110g / 1 cup redcurrants
4oz / 110g / 1 cup blackcurrants
4oz / 110g / 1 cup small strawberries
4oz / 110g / 1 cup blueberries
4oz / 110g / 1 cup fraises du bois or wild strawberries

For the syrup:
14oz / 400g / 2 cups sugar
³/4 pint / 450ml / 2 cups water
6-8 large sweet geranium leaves

Place the berries in a white china or glass bowl. Put the sugar, water and sweet geranium leaves into a stainless steel saucepan and bring slowly to the boil, stirring until the sugar dissolves. Boil for just 2 minutes. Cool for 4-5 minutes, then pour the hot syrup over the fruit and allow to macerate for several hours. Remove the geranium leaves. Serve chilled, garnished with a few fresh geranium leaves, with softly-whipped cream or vanilla ice-cream, or alone.

Variation - Summer Berry Jelly with Sweet Geranium Leaves:
If there is some berry salad left over, particularly if there is more juice than fruit, it can be made into a jelly: measure the juices and use 4 teaspoons of gelatine to each 1 pint / 600ml / 2¹/2 cups of liquid. You'll need 2 pints / 1.2 litres / 5 cups for a large ring mould. Turn it out carefully onto a large white china plate when it is set, fill the centre with softly whipped cream and decorate with geranium leaves.

Barberstown Castle

Straffan, Co Kildare

One of the few houses in the area to have been occupied continuously for over four centuries, Barberstown Castle is steeped in history through three very different periods. The oldest part is very much a real castle - the original keep in the middle section of the building was built by a Nicholas Barby in the early 13th century - and this was followed by a more domestic Elizabethan house, added in the second half of the 16th century. Hugh Barton (also associated with nearby Straffan House, now the Kildare Hotel & Country Club, with which Barberstown shares golf and leisure facilities) then built the 'new' Victorian wing in the 1830s - and, most recently, this immaculately maintained property was considerably extended to include a luxurious new bedroom wing; however, this has been carefully planned to match the older sections of the castle, and an ongoing sense of history remains one of its most powerful attractions.

Wild mushroom and red onion tart with thyme crème fraîche

Durrus is a semi-soft washed rind Irish farmhouse cheese made in West Cork; it has a rich flavour and melts beautifully. This makes a delicious starter, or a light lunch or supper dish.

Serves 4
1 tub of crème fraîche
a few sprigs of thyme
3 medium red onions
2 tbsp / 3 US tablespoons olive oil
2oz / 50g / ½ stick butter
9oz / 250g wild mushrooms
1 clove garlic,
1 tbsp / 1¼ US tablespoons parsley, chopped
1lb / 450g puff pastry
1 x 13oz / 380g Durrus Cheese
salt & freshly ground black pepper
Garnish:
1 bag of rocket
a few chive leaves, chopped
a little extra virgin olive oil

Preheat a moderate oven, 350°F / 180°C / gas mark 4.

To prepare the topping: Strip the leaves from one or two of the thyme sprigs, then chop them and mix with 4 tablespoons / 5 US tablespoons of the crème fraîche, and a seasoning of salt and freshly ground pepper. Peel the red onions and cut into medium slices, then cook slowly in a saucepan with half of the olive oil and butter until soft. Pan fry the mushrooms in the remaining oil and butter, adding in the chopped garlic and parsley when they are cooked.

To make the tart: Roll out the pastry to about ¼ inch / 0.5 cm in thickness. Using a side plate as a guide, cut into 4 circles. Prick the centre of each pastry circle several times with a fork. Place a quarter of the onion in the centre of each circle, then place the wild mushrooms on top, followed by a sprig of thyme, then a generous tablespoon of the crème fraiche in the centre and finish with three generous slices of Durrus Cheese. Line a large baking tray with grease-proof paper and bake in the preheated oven for 15 to 20 minutes.

To serve: Garnish the top with a little rocket and chive salad, and drizzle with extra virgin olive oil.

Banana bread

At Barberstown Castle, fresh banana bread is served with tea and coffee throughout the day and is a favourite with regular guests.

Makes 2 loaves
18oz / 500g ripe banana, chopped
18oz / 500g / 2¹/₄ cups sugar
18oz / 500g / 1¹/₃ cup white flour
¹/₂oz / 15g baking powder
9oz / 250g / 2¹/₂ sticks unsalted
   butter, softened
6 eggs
finely grated zest of 1 washed lemon
a dash of vanilla essence
a good dash of rum

Preheat a moderate oven, 350°F / 180°C / gas mark 4.

Grease two 2 lb / 450g loaf tins or terrines, and lay a sheet of greaseproof paper on the base. In a large bowl, mix the banana and sugar together. When well mixed, gradually blend in the flour and baking powder, sifted together, then mix in the butter in small cubes. Add the eggs, one by one, mixing well after each addition. Finally, mix in the lemon zest, vanilla extract and rum. Turn into the tins and smooth the tops.

Bake in the preheated oven for 35 minutes, then reduce the oven temperature to 325°F / 160°C / gas mark 3 and bake for a further 25 minutes or until well-risen, lightly browned and springy to the touch. Cool the loaves on a wire rack and served sliced, with tea or coffee.

Belle Isle Castle

Lisbellaw, Co Fermanagh

Magically situated on one of eleven islands owned by the Duke of Abercorn on Upper Lough Erne, this aptly named castle dates back to 1680 and has mid-19th century additions. Under the hospitable supervision of hosts Charles and Fiona Plunket, Belle Isle has a delightfully exclusive away-from-it-all country house atmosphere and is impressively furnished with antiques, striking paintings and dramatic colour schemes (the work of the internationally renowned interior designer, David Hicks); and, in addition to the eight romantic bedrooms, which all have their special character, guests have use of a magnificent drawing room and also the Grand Hall, complete with minstrels' gallery, where dinner is served. There are many wonderful things to do in this idyllically beautiful area - fishing, of course, but also field sports, and golf, and there are historic houses and gardens to visit nearby. But, most tempting of all, perhaps, might be a visit to their own Belle Isle School of Cookery, which offers an extensive range of courses throughout the year.

Belle Isle blackberry mousse

This dessert has the most wonderful colour and flavour, and is a favourite at Belle Isle, where the Plunket family love blackberrying - and Charles (unlike the rest of the family, including the black labrador, Finnegan) manages to pick pounds without eating any! In Ireland, blackberries are there for the taking in country hedges in September and they freeze well - simply spread out on a plastic tray and transfer to bags when frozen. This mousse loses none of its flavour when using frozen fruit.

Serves 4-6
1lb / 450g / 2 cups blackberries, fresh
* or frozen and defrosted*
juice of a small lemon, strained
4oz / 100g / 1/2 cup caster sugar
3 tbsp / 4 US tablespoons cold water
1/2oz / 15g powdered gelatine
1/4pt / 150ml / 3/4 cup double cream
2 egg whites
To serve:
1/4pt / 150ml / 3/4 cup single cream
a few sprigs of mint
a few raw blackberries

Wash and pick over the blackberries and place in a saucepan with the strained lemon juice and the sugar. Place over a low heat, cover and simmer gently for about 10 minutes. Meanwhile, put the water in a basin, sprinkle in the gelatine and leave to soak for 5 minutes. Draw the pan off the heat, add the soaked gelatine and stir until dissolved. Pass the fruit and juice through a nylon sieve, into a large basin. Rub as much of the fruit through as possible and discard the pips left in the sieve. Set the purée aside until cool and beginning to set. Beat the egg whites until stiff, and lightly whip the cream.

Using a metal soon, gently fold the cream and the egg whites into the purée until well blended, losing as little volume as possible. Pour the mixture into a serving dish or into individual serving bowls. Chill until set. Serve garnished with a few whole blackberries and a sprig of mint, and offer a little extra pouring cream.

Broad bean and coriander soup

This simple soup has a really unusual flavour and is especially delicious when made with small, freshly picked home-grown broad beans although, when unavailable, frozen beans may be used instead.

Serves 4

1oz / 25g / 2 tablespoons butter
1 medium onion, finely sliced
8 oz / 250g / 1¼ cups shelled broad beans, thawed if frozen
1 pint / 600ml / 2¾ cups hot vegetable stock
2 tbsp / 2½ US tablespoons medium dry sherry
4 tbsp / 5 US tablespoons Greek yoghurt
3 tbsp / 3¾ US tablespoons chopped, fresh coriander leaves
salt & freshly ground pepper

Melt the butter in a heavy-based saucepan and add the thinly sliced onion. Cover and cook gently for about five minutes until the onion is soft and transparent.

Add the beans and stock. Cover and simmer for 20 minutes. Remove from the heat, allow to cool a little, and pour into a blender. Add the sherry, yoghurt, chopped coriander and a seasoning of salt and freshly ground pepper, then blend until just smooth.

Reheat gently and serve immediately with freshly baked wheaten (wholemeal) or brown bread.

Belle Isle School of Cookery

Lisbellaw, Co Fermanagh

In a fine kitchen overlooking the Florencecourt Mountains, the chef-manager of Belle Isle School of Cookery, Liz Moore, adopts a modern approach to cooking. Throughout all the courses, which range from one day to four weeks, it is her philosophy to show how local produce can be dramatically transformed when contemporary ideas are mingled with traditional Irish recipes.

Iced red fruits with hot white chocolate sauce

An incredibly simple pudding - it is hard to believe that it can be so easy to make, yet taste so good. The sauce is best served at the table so it can be really hot before folding in the frozen berries.

Serves 4

8oz / 225g / 1 cup frozen small summer berries – raspberries, small strawberries, red currants.
1/2 pint / 300ml / 1 1/3 cup cream
8oz / 225g white chocolate, broken into small pieces.
mint leaves, to garnish

Remove the fruit from the freezer no more than 10-12 minutes before serving. (If you take it out earlier the fruit will have thawed completely, and it needs to have a bit of a bite). Heat the cream gently in a small saucepan and watch carefully; when you notice bubbles at the side of the pan, turn off the heat.

Break the chocolate into pieces and add to the cream, stirring, until the chocolate has melted. Remove from the heat, seal the saucepan with cling film and cover it with a lid to keep the sauce warm. Divide the frozen fruit between four bowls or glasses and allow it to defrost slightly. Just before serving, pour the hot sauce over the fruit, and garnish with a sprig of mint. The fruit should be slightly thawed and the sauce hot. This also looks particularly pretty in an ice bowl. This is made by putting one bowl inside another bowl, securing, filling the gap between the bowls with water and freezing. In this case serve the sauce separately in a jug.

Tuna carpaccio

A great starter or lunch dish because it is so light and fresh. Use wild salmon instead of tuna during the season. The dressing must go on just before serving, but the fish may be sliced an hour or so beforehand, covered, and kept in the fridge until required.

Serves 4
1 lb / 450g fresh tuna or wild salmon
4 tbsp / 5 US tablespoons olive oil or hazelnut oil
2 tbsp / 2¹/₂ US tablespoons lemon juice
2 tsp whole grain mustard
2 tsp fresh thyme or basil, finely chopped
salt and freshly ground pepper
1 small red onion, very finely sliced
watercress to garnish

First make the dressing: In a bowl, combine the oil, lemon juice, mustard and herbs. Season to taste.

The fish must be very fresh. Slice as thinly as possible, with a sharp knife.

To serve: Lay the fish out attractively on four serving plates, sprinkle with the red onion and, just before serving, spoon over a generous amount of dressing. Garnish simply with the watercress and serve with home-made brown bread.

Blairs Cove House

Durrus, Co Cork

This lovely Georgian house enjoys a stunning waterside location near Bantry, at the head of Dunmanus Bay. An elegant conservatory which is particularly attractive on fine summer evenings overlooks the central courtyard, while the main dining room - which was once a stable block - is lofty, stone-walled and black-beamed, with a magnificent chandelier as a central feature, gilt-framed family portraits on the walls and a grand piano, where an irresistible array of desserts is displayed. An enormous central buffet groans under the weight of the hors d'oeuvre display, a speciality that is unrivalled in Ireland and, along with the piano-top desserts, has become a trademark. Main course specialities of local seafood or the best of meat and poultry are char-grilled at a special wood-fired grill right in the restaurant and, of course, full justice is done to the ever-growing selection of local farmhouses cheese for which West Cork is rightly renowned. Luxurious, individualistic accommodation is also offered.

Brandade of cod

This purée of salted cod can be eaten cold as part of a starter selection - it features regularly in the famous Blairs Cove hors d'oeuvre display - or warm as a main course, with vegetables.

Serves 4 as a starter
1 lb / 450g cod, filleted
salt
6 fl oz / 175ml / ⁴/₅ cup cream
3 cloves of garlic
5fl oz / 150ml / ³/₄ cup olive oil
pepper and lemon juice to taste

Cover the raw cod fillet with a thick layer of salt and refrigerate overnight. Rinse and soak in fresh water for 1 hour. Remove the skin and bones, then put the fish into fresh water, bring to the boil and simmer for 5 minutes. Drain well. Put into a food processor.

Put the cream into a saucepan with the garlic and oil, and bring gently up to the boil. Simmer to soften the garlic, then add to the fish and blend until just smooth. Season with pepper and lemon juice.

To serve as a starter, chill the brandade in the fridge then scoop into quenelle shapes and arrange on plates with grilled peppers, fennel and olives.

Alternatively serve lukewarm as a main course, with new potatoes and a green salad.

Lemon and almond tart

This classic tart makes a regular appearance among the famous display of desserts on the grand piano at Blairs Cove.

Serves 6-8

8oz / 225g short crust pastry, home made (4 oz / 110g / 1 cup flour etc) or commercial
2 eggs
5oz / 150g / 1¹/₅ cups icing sugar
4 lemons
4oz / 100g / 1 stick butter, melted
3oz / 75g / ³/₅ cup ground almonds

Pre-heat a hot oven, 400°F / 200°C / gas mark 6.

Line an 8 inch / 20 cm tart tin with the short crust pastry and bake blind. (To bake blind, prick the pastry base with a fork, line with greaseproof paper and a scattering of baking beans, then bake for about 10 minutes, or until the pastry case has set and is lightly coloured, taking out the paper and beans shortly before removing the pastry case from the oven). Set the prepared case aside, and reduce the oven temperature to 350°F / 180°C / gas mark 4.

In a bowl, whisk the eggs and icing sugar together until pale and fluffy. Wash and dry two of the lemons, finely grate the zest and mix it into the egg mixture with the butter, ground almonds and the juice of all four lemons. Don't worry if the mixture looks curdled, it won't affect the final result.

Pour the filling into the pastry case and bake for 25 minutes at 350°F/ 180°C / gas mark 4, or until set. Serve warm or cold, decorated with a few slivers of lemon zest and a light sprinkling of icing sugar.

The Bushmills Inn

Bushmills, Co Antrim

Established as a coaching inn in the 19th century, this well-loved hotel is just a couple of miles from the Giant's Causeway - and only a few hundred yards from the world's oldest distillery. The inn has grown in recent years, but its development under the current ownership has been thoughtful, and none of its original old-world character has been lost. A wing quite recently added was so skilfully designed that it is hard to see where the old ends and the new begins - and inside, too, all the features which made the old Inn special have been carried through and blended with new amenities. The tone is set by the turf fire and country seating in the hall, and public rooms – bars, the famous circular library, the restaurant, even the Pine Room conference room – carry on the same theme: a comfortable cottage style prevails throughout.

Dalriada cullen skink

This traditional dish is named after the ancient kingdom of Dalriada, which straddled the Irish Sea taking in both Ayrshire in Scotland and the north coast of County Antrim. And, while it can be a superb soup in Scotland, at the Bushmills Inn it is a dish "out on its own". It's a real meal in a soup bowl, especially when served with the optional poached egg garnish.

Serves 4

2 skinless fillets of natural smoked haddock

12 baby potatoes, boiled and sliced into thirds

A little butter for frying

1 bunch of scallions (spring onions), roughly chopped

For the fish cream:

6 shallots finely diced

1/2 oz / 20g / 2 US tablespoons butter

1/4 pint / 150ml / 3/4 cup dry white wine

1 pint / 600ml / 2 3/4 cups good fish stock

1 pint / 600ml / 2 3/4 cups double cream

a few strands of saffron

Garnish:

4 poached eggs (optional)

First make the fish cream: Sweat the shallots in the butter over a medium heat until soft. Increase the heat and add the wine, then boil to reduce by about a third (enough to drive off the alcohol). Add the stock and simmer gently, until it has reduced by half again. Finish by adding the cream and saffron, and allow the sauce to thicken over a low heat.

Cut the smoked haddock fillets in half and place in a heavy-based pan. Pour the fish cream over and poach for 5-8 minutes, depending on their size. Meanwhile, sauté the potato slices in a little butter and toss with a scattering of scallions.

To serve: Place 6-8 slices of potato in the centre of a large soup plate, then carefully lift out the haddock fillets from their poaching liquor, and place on top. A poached egg can also be added, if you like. Spoon a little of the fish cream around the outside and garnish with the remaining scallions.

Armagh apple tartlets with caramel sauce

A caramelised apple tart inspired by the "Orchard of Ireland" - County Armagh. Brandy could be used instead of Calvados, if preferred.

Serves 4
For the tartlet:
3-4 eating apples
4 thin rounds puff pastry,
    approximately 6 inch / 15 cm in
    diameter
1oz / 25g / 2 US tablespoons unsalted
    butter, melted
a little icing sugar
For the frangipane:
3oz / 75g / 3/4 stick unsalted butter,
    very soft
3oz / 75g / 1/3 cup caster sugar
1 large egg, beaten
4oz / 110g / 1 cup ground almonds
1oz / 25g / 2 US tablespoons plain
    flour
1/2fl oz / 15 ml / 1 US tablespoons
    milk
a dash of Calvados
For the caramel sauce:
14oz / 400g / 1 3/4 cups caster sugar
16fl oz / 500 ml / 2 1/4 cups cold
    water
16fl oz / 500 ml / 2 1/4 cups cream
Garnish:
a little crème fraîche
fresh mint leaves

Preheat a moderately hot oven, 350°F / 180°C / gas mark 4.

First make the frangipane: Beat the butter and sugar till light and fluffy, then fold in the egg, ground almonds, flour, milk and finally the Calvados. Chill in the fridge until required.

To make the pastry bases: Place the puff pastry discs onto a floured baking tray and prick with a fork, then bake in the pre-heated oven 8-10 minutes or until golden brown and slightly rising. While still warm, and to keep the disc quite flat, place another baking sheet on top and push down slightly to expel the air from the pastry.

For the caramel sauce: In a heavy-based pan, heat the sugar and water gently until it forms a rich golden coloured syrup. Remove from heat and allow to cool slightly, then heat the cream and carefully add to the syrup. Return to the heat for a few seconds; strain through a fine sieve if necessary.

To complete: Arrange the cooled pastry discs on a baking sheet and spread a layer of the frangipane on each one, leaving a narrow margin around the edge. Peel, core and thinly slice the apples and arrange neatly on top of the tarts; brush with melted butter and bake for 10-12 minutes. Finally, dust the tart with icing sugar and place under the grill until the sugar starts to caramelise.

To serve: Place the tartlets on warmed dessert plates and drizzle the caramel sauce around them. Garnish with a little crème fraîche and a sprig of mint, and finally dust with icing sugar.

Caragh Lodge

Caragh Lake, Co Kerry

Lush, nestling and hospitable, Mary Gaunt's lovely Victorian house is an idyllic place, with views of Ireland's highest mountains, the McGillicuddy Reeks, and it's a lovely spot for swimming or boating as well as salmon and trout fishing. The gardens run right down to the shores of that startlingly beautiful little gem, Caragh Lake, and the house - which is elegantly furnished with antiques but not too formal - makes a cool, restful retreat. Mary has a real love of cooking and local produce such as freshly caught seafood, often including wild salmon from Caragh Lake, Kerry lamb and home-grown vegetables, takes pride of place at dinners served in the classically proportioned dining room overlooking the lake. Baking is a particular strength, not only in delicious home-baked breads, but also baked desserts and treats for afternoon tea that include recipes handed down in her family through generations. Comfortable accommodation is divided between the original rooms in the main house and an attractive new wing which has its own entrance, sitting room and open fire - and rooms stylishly furnished in an upbeat traditional style.

Braised lamb shanks
with minted pea purée

In Kerry the lambs graze on the natural and varied flora of the mountain pastures, giving them great flavour. Braising lamb shanks turns an inexpensive cut of meat into a feast, and this dish is deservedly popular with guests at Caragh Lodge.

Serves 4
4 lamb shanks
4 tbsp / 5 US tablespoons olive oil
2 large carrots, peeled and roughly
*   chopped*
2 onions, peeled and chopped
1 large stick celery, chopped
2 parsnips, peeled and chopped
1 large clove garlic, peeled and
*   halved*
1 x 14 oz / 400g tin of tomatoes
20fl oz / 600ml / 2³/₄ cups red wine
20fl oz / 600ml / 2³/₄ cups beef stock
2 bay leaves
4 sprigs fresh rosemary
sea salt and freshly ground black
*   pepper*

Minted pea and potato purée:
2 large potatoes, unpeeled
2oz / 50g / ¹/₂ stick butter
6fl oz / 175ml / ⁴/₅ cup cream
sea salt and freshly ground black
*   pepper*
1lb / 450g / 2¹/₄ cups fresh or frozen
*   peas*
2 tbsp / 2¹/₂ US tablespoons fresh
*   mint, chopped*

Preheat a very cool oven, 275°F / 140°C / gas mark 1.

Season the lamb shanks with salt and freshly ground black pepper. Heat the oil in a casserole and, when it is really hot, brown the shanks on all sides. Remove from the casserole and reserve. Add the vegetables to the casserole and brown them on all sides for about 6 minutes or until nicely browned. Add the garlic, tomatoes, wine, stock, bay leaves, rosemary and some seasoning. Place lamb shanks on top and bring gently up to a simmer, then cover the casserole with a lid and transfer it to the oven, to braise slowly for 3 hours or until the meat is very tender and almost falling off the bones. Remove the lamb shanks and keep warm. Continue to simmer the sauce uncovered for 10 minutes, or until reduced and thickened, then strain and discard the flavouring vegetables. Return the shanks to the pan and check the sauce for seasoning.

To make the pea purée: Boil the potatoes in their jackets until soft. Drain, cool slightly, then peel and mash well. Return to the saucepan and add the butter, cream and a seasoning of salt and pepper. Reheat, whisking until smooth. Keep warm. Cook the peas in a little lightly salted water for 5 minutes, or until tender. Drain. Put the peas, mint and a few spoonfuls of the potato mixture into a blender and process until smooth. Add to the remaining potato and stir over low heat until hot.

To serve: Divide the minted pea purée between four warm plates. Place the lamb shanks on top and pour the sauce over.

Fig & pine nut log with honeyed walnuts, and rosemary & oatmeal biscuits

At Caragh Lodge Mary Gaunt offers a cheese plate that includes several Killorglin cheeses, made at Wilma and John O'Connor's farm nearby - served with home-made biscuits, and this unusual fruit and nut 'salami' to accompany.

Serves 6-8
14oz / 400g / 2^1/$_4$ cups dried figs, roughly chopped
1 small glass of port
2oz / 50g / ^{1}/$_2$ cup pine nuts, toasted
Honeyed walnuts:
2oz / 50g / ^{1}/$_2$ cup walnuts
4fl oz / 100 ml / ^{1}/$_3$ cup of honey
3 cardamom pods, crushed
Rosemary & oatmeal biscuits:
5oz / 150g / 1^1/$_4$ cups wholemeal flour
3oz / 75g / ^{3}/$_4$ cup oatflakes
4 tsp brown sugar
1 tsp baking powder
1 tsp sea salt
1 tsp dried rosemary leaves, crumbled
4oz / 100g / 1 stick butter
a little milk to mix
paprika for sprinkling

Fig and pine nut log: Soak the figs overnight in the port. Drain off any excess, then combine six figs and half of the pine nuts in a blender and process until smooth. Stir in the remaining figs and pine nuts, and knead and shape into a long log. Wrap the log tightly in cling film and put in the freezer until firm enough to slice.

Honeyed walnuts: Lightly toast the walnuts in a pan. Add the honey and cardamoms and gently heat through. Remove from the heat and allow to cool. When cool remove the cardamoms and discard.

Preheat a moderate oven, 350°F / 180°C / gas mark 4

Biscuits: Combine the flour, oatflakes, sugar, baking powder, salt and rosemary. Rub in the butter until the mixture resembles fine breadcrumbs. Add just enough milk to form a dough. Turn out onto a floured board, knead lightly into shape then roll out thinly. Using a round cookie cutter, cut out circles and place on a greased baking tray. Sprinkle lightly with paprika and bake in the preheated oven for about 15-20 minutes, or until light golden brown. Cool on a wire rack. When completely cold store in an airtight tin.

To serve: Cut the log into slices and serve with the honeyed walnuts, the biscuits and a selection of cheeses.

Cashel House Hotel

Cashel, Co Galway

Secluded in a 40-acre estate of flowering shrubs and woodland walks, Cashel House Hotel is quietly located at the head of Cashel Bay and was formerly one of Connemara's most gracious private residences. Kay and Dermot McEvilly opened Cashel House as an hotel in 1968 and were among the first Irish Country House proprietors to welcome guests to their home. When they hosted General and Madame de Gaulle for two weeks in the following year, they played a key role in the development of Ireland as a gourmet destination for discerning travellers, as that historic visit put the Gallic seal of approval on the combination of Irish hospitality and good, simple food that was just emerging at the time. Other family members have since joined Dermot and Kay at Cashel House and it remains one of the great strengths of the Irish country house movement, offering a very high standard of comfort and service enhanced by good sense and a refreshingly down to earth attitude, especially where food is concerned: delicious local produce is abundant, and they treat it with respect

Warm Cashel mussels
with garlic, tomato and chilli

Guests at Cashel love to have seafood from the area, and this unusual dish is understandably popular. The mussels are picked from the rocks in Cashel Bay in the morning and used for dinner the same evening - it is very important to use mussels on the day they are picked, so check with your fishmonger. This would be perfect for a dinner party starter, or a light lunch.

Serves 6
6¹/₂ lb / 3kg mussels, approx.
olive oil
3 cloves of garlic, peeled and finely
  chopped
1 green chilli, finely chopped
1 red chilli, finely chopped
1 x 14 oz / 400g tin plum tomatoes
1/2 pint / 300ml / 1¹/₃ cups lager
2 scallions (spring onions), cut into
  strips

First wash the mussels in plenty of cold water; scrub well and remove the beards; use only mussels which are tightly closed, discarding any that are open.

In a large pan, heat some olive oil and sauté the garlic in it to soften a little without browning. Add the mussels and cook for 5 minutes (or just until the shells are opening), then add the chopped chillis and the tomatoes. Cook for a further 3 minutes to heat through, then finally add the lager and cook for a further 2 minutes or until the broth reaches boiling point. Serve in large bowls topped with sliced scallions, and accompany with home-made brown bread.

Mary's boiled fruit cake

This is a lovely moist cake which would be lovely for afternoon tea or packed in with a picnic lunch. It keeps very well for up to 3 months.

Makes one 8 inch / 20 cm diameter cake

8oz / 225g / 2¼ sticks butter
1 bottle / 300ml / 1⅓ cups Guinness (stout)
8oz / 225g / 1 cup brown sugar
1lb / 450g / 3 cups raisins
1lb / 450g / 3 cups sultanas
4oz / 110g / 1 cup candied peel
12oz / 350g / 3 cups plain white flour
1 tsp bicarbonate of soda (bread soda)
1 tsp allspice
4 eggs

Line a deep 8 inch / 20 cm cake tin with buttered greaseproof paper.

Put the butter, Guinness, sugar, raisins, sultanas and candied peel in a heavy bottomed saucepan. Bring slowly up to the boil, stirring to dissolve the sugar. Boil for about 10 minutes. Then remove from heat, turn into a mixing bowl and leave to cool until it is warm rather than hot.

Meanwhile, preheat a warm oven, 325°F / 165°C / gas mark 3.

When the fruit and Guinness mixture has cooled enough, sift together the flour, bread soda and allspice. Beat the eggs lightly, then slowly add half of the eggs to the fruit and Guinness mixture. Next, fold in some of the flour, and add the remaining eggs and the flour mixture, folding gently all the time until all is incorporated and thoroughly mixed, with no flour showing. Turn into the prepared tin, smooth the top and bake in the preheated oven for 2 hours or until nicely browned and springy to the touch. To check if the cake is ready, test with a skewer, which will come out clean when it is cooked. Remove from oven and allow to cool in the tin; turn out when cold, then wrap in greaseproof paper and store in an airtight tin until required.

Castle Durrow

Durrow, Co Laois

This impressive 18th century country house halfway between Dublin and Cork has some magnificent features and spacious, luxurious accommodation in individually decorated guest rooms and suites. Those in the main house have views over the surrounding parkland and countryside, while newer rooms in an adjacent wing are on the ground floor, overlooking a formal courtyard and near the old walled garden, which is under restoration. A large marbled reception hall is welcoming with fresh flowers, and candles are lit after dark, giving the whole area, including the adjacent Castle Restaurant - a gently contemporary dining room, with a pleasantly bright, pastoral outlook in daytime, candlelit at night - a lovely romantic feeling. Careful sourcing of all food is the policy here and local produce is used where possible: the walled garden is now supplying the kitchen with some seasonal produce, including herbs and salads - and the cheese plate might include Lavistown cheese, a fine handmade product from nearby Kilkenny.

Avocado and smoked chicken salad

This dish is a subtle blend of Asian and Irish influences - guests at Castle Durrow love the modern take on chicken and avocado.

Serves 4 as a starter,
2 as a light meal

1 little gem lettuce cut in half and sliced thinly

5 oz / 150g / 3 cups bean sprouts

2 ripe avocados, peeled, halved, stones removed, and sliced lengthways

2 smoked chicken breasts, sliced lengthways

3 oz / 80g / 1 cup baby corn blanched, refreshed and halved lengthways

7oz / 200g / 2 cups shiitake mushrooms, cleaned and fried in a little sesame oil

1 punnet mustard cress

1 tbsp black sesame seeds

1 tbsp glutinous rice, dry roasted and ground in a mortar and pestle to a fine powder

Lime dressing:

1 clove garlic, peeled

20 sprigs coriander

pinch of sea salt

1 green chilli

4 limes, juiced

1 tbsp / 1¼ US tablespoons soy sauce

1 small shallot, diced

1 tbsp / 1¼ US tablespoons fish sauce

1 tbsp yellow lump sugar (palm sugar), or caster sugar

First make the dressing: Place the garlic, coriander and salt in a mortar and pestle, and pound to a paste. Add the chilli and crush slightly, then add the rest of the ingredients and mix lightly until the sugar is fully incorporated. Leave to rest for about 20 minutes to allow the flavours to develop.

To complete the dish: Dress the lettuce and bean sprouts in a little of the lime dressing, and lay out on four plates. Arrange the avocado, smoked chicken and baby corn into layers; sprinkle with a little soy sauce, and top with mustard cress. Arrange the shitake mushrooms around the plate and pour some of the lime dressing over them. Sprinkle with black sesame seeds and the ground rice.

Castle Durrow chocolate brownies

A treat for afternoon tea, or with coffee after dinner.

Makes enough for two swiss roll
tins (about 2 dozen brownies)
6oz / 175g / 1³/₄ sticks butter
8oz / 255g dark chocolate
3 eggs
6oz / 175g / ³/₄ cups caster sugar
6oz / 175g / 1¹/₃ cups plain white
flour
1 tsp / 5g baking powder
2oz / 50g / ¹/₃ cup cocoa powder
2oz / 50g / ¹/₂ cup pecan nuts,
chopped
2oz / 50g / ¹/₃ cup hazelnuts,
chopped

Preheat a moderate oven, 350°F / 175°C / gas mark 4.

Line two baking trays with silicon (non-stick) paper.

Melt the butter and chocolate together over a basin of simmering water. Meanwhile whisk the eggs and sugar until doubled in volume. Sieve together the flour, baking powder and cocoa powder. Gently mix the chocolate and butter into the egg mixture, then fold in the sieved flour mixture and, finally, the nuts.

Divide the mixture between the trays and bake for 10 minutes, then turn the heat down to 300°F / 150°C / gas mark 2 and bake for another 8 minutes. Leave to cool in the trays. Cut into squares when cold, and store in an airtight tin.

Castle Leslie

Glaslough, Co Monaghan

During its three centuries in the Leslie family, this extraordinary place has changed remarkably little - and its fascinating history intrigues guests as much as the eccentricity of Castle Leslie as they find it today. Once inside the massive front door (guarded by family dogs who snooze in beds flanking the stone steps) you will find no phones, television sets or clocks in the rooms, although generous heating and plentiful hot water allow full appreciation of the wonders of Victorian plumbing. In a charming reverse of circumstances, the family lives in the servants' wing, allowing guests to enjoy the castle to the full – it has all the original furniture and family portraits. Dinner in the castle is done in fine old style, served by waitresses wearing Victorian uniforms, in rooms that include the original dining room, unchanged for over a century. (The Hunting Lodge & Castle Leslie Equestrian Centre, on the estate, offer less formal dining.) Yet, despite the faded grandeur, executive chef Noel McMeel, headed up by Gary McDowell at the Castle, offers modern Irish cooking. There's also a Castle Leslie range of preserves and speciality foods - and even a cookery school in the old kitchen.

Fillet of Irish Angus beef with fondant potatoes, salsa verde and red wine & rosemary jus

Great pride is taken in the quality of all ingredients at Castle Leslie, and only the finest Angus beef is used for steaks.

Serves 4

4 x 10oz / 275g fillet steaks, at room
    temperature

For the jus:

1 sprig fresh rosemary
1 onion, roughly cut
4 garlic cloves
a few root vegetables, roughly cut
1 bottle of red wine
3^1/$_2$ pints / 2 litres / 9 cups good
    quality beef stock

For the fondant potatoes:

4 large potatoes
1^3/$_4$ pints / 1 litre / 4^1/$_2$ cups chicken
    stock
11oz / 300g / 3 sticks butter
salt and black pepper

For the salsa verde:

15 mint leaves
2 handfuls flat leaf parsley
15 basil leaves
1 garlic clove crushed
1 tbsp / 1^1/$_4$ US tablespoons drained
    capers
1 tbsp / 1^1/$_4$ US tablespoons Dijon
    mustard
3 anchovy fillets
1 tbsp / 1^1/$_4$ US tablespoons Red wine
    vinegar
200ml / ^{4}/$_5$ cup olive oil

First make the jus: Heat a large saucepan until very hot, then add the rosemary, onion, garlic, and root vegetables along with the red wine and reduce by four fifths. Then add the beef stock and continue to reduce until it has made a nice glaze with a good deep colour. Keep warm until required.

Next prepare the potatoes: Preheat a fairly hot oven 375°F / 190°C / gas mark 5. Peel the potatoes, slice into discs and rinse in cold water. Drain and put into a flameproof casserole with the chicken stock and the butter. Bring to the boil over direct heat, then place in the preheated oven and continue cooking for around 20 minutes or until the potatoes are tender.

To make the salsa verde: Place all the ingredients except the oil into a liquidiser and purée, then slowly add the olive oil until the herbs and oil form a paste. Refrigerate until required.

To cook the steaks: Lightly oil the steaks and season them with freshly ground black pepper. Heat a frying pan until very hot and place the beef fillets in and seal on all sides until golden, then cook to your requirements. (Medium rare is recommended. As cooking time depends on thickness not weight, it is advisable to test by touch: if the flesh feels soft it is rare, if it resists a little it is medium rare; well done steak is firm to the touch.)

To assemble the dish: Divide the fondant potato between four warmed plates, then place the steaks on top; using two dessert spoons, make a quenelle of the salsa verde and place this on top of the steak. Drizzle the jus around the plate and serve immediately.

Pan fried scallops with black pudding and red pepper marmalade

The exclusive range of food products made at Castle Leslie includes some unusual preserves and condiments, such as the Hot Tomato & Chilli Jam that is served with this attractive starter.

Serves 4
12 slices of good quality black
    pudding
12 scallops, with coral removed
For the red pepper marmalade:
2 red peppers
1 red onion, finely diced
300ml / 1/2 pint / 1 1/3 cups white wine
    vinegar
200g / 7 oz / 4/5 cup caster sugar
To serve:
Castle Leslie hot tomato and chilli jam

First prepare the red pepper marmalade: Preheat a fairly hot grill. Coat the peppers lightly in oil, then set them under the grill until the skin blisters and starts to turn black. Place the peppers in a polythene bag and allow to sweat until the skin comes off easily. When the skin is removed, cut into julienne (thin strips) and add the finely chopped onion, then place in a stainless steel saucepan along with the vinegar and caster sugar. Set over moderate heat, uncovered, and allow to reduce and caramelise.

To cook the black pudding & scallops: Heat a little oil in a frying pan, and fry the black pudding lightly in it on both sides. Heat another frying pan with a little oil, and seal the scallops in it briefly on both sides, just until they are a nice golden colour on the outside.

To assemble the dish: Place three pieces of the black pudding on each warmed plate, then place the scallops on top, and finish off with the red pepper marmalade. Finally, drizzle some of the Castle Leslie hot tomato and chilli jam on the plate and serve immediately.

Chapter One Restaurant

Parnell Square, Dublin 1

In an arched basement beneath the Irish Writers Museum, one of Ireland's finest restaurants is to be found in the former home of the great John Jameson of whiskey fame. Joint proprietors Ross Lewis and Martin Corbett have earned an enviable reputation here, both for Ross's imaginative modern Irish cooking with an emphasis on seasonal organic and specialist produce and, under Martin's supervision, for superb service from friendly and well-informed staff. The original granite walls and old brickwork of this fine Georgian house contrast with elegant modern decor to create atmospheric surroundings, and special features include a beautiful carved oyster counter in the reception area, where you can choose the perfect bubbly from their champagne menu to accompany the noble bivalve. Impeccably sourced ingredients are at the heart of this fine kitchen and Ross's cooking - classic French lightly tempered by modern influences - showcases specialist Irish produce whenever possible, notably on a magnificent charcuterie trolley, which is a treat not to be missed. Another special treat is the brilliantly timed pre-theatre menu, for which they are rightly renowned: depart for one of the nearby theatres after your main course, and return for dessert after the performance. Perfect timing, every time.

Roast monkfish with celeriac, red wine sauce and champ

The monkfish and the bacon make a classic partnership in this hearty speciality from Chapter One. Although it is very much a chef's creation, don't be too daunted by the long list of ingredients or the number of stages; each section is quite simple to complete, and what you get here is several dishes in one recipe.

Serves 4
For the red wine sauce:
4 shallots
2 oz / 50g / 1 cup mushrooms, sliced
2 tbsp / 10ml light olive oil
$^1/_2$ pint / 300 ml / 1$^1/_3$ cups red wine
14fl oz / 400ml chicken stock
a sprig each of: thyme, rosemary,
    parsley, tarragon & 1 bay leaf
5 black peppercorns
4fl oz / 100 ml / $^1/_2$ cup double cream
1 tbsp unsalted butter
salt & freshly ground white pepper
For the champ:
4 medium-sized Rooster potatoes
7fl oz / 200ml / 1 cup cream
3oz / 80g / $^3/_4$ stick butter, chilled and
    cubed
8 scallions (spring onions), chopped
salt, freshly ground white pepper and
    a pinch of nutmeg
For the celeriac:
14fl oz / 400 ml / 2 cups milk and
    water, in equal parts
1 head of celeriac, trimmed & cut
    into $^3/_4$ inch / 2 cm dice
4 fl oz / 100ml / $^1/_2$ cup cream,
    approx.
a little Dijon mustard
1-2 tbsp chives, chopped
salt & freshly ground white pepper.
For the monkfish:
4 x 6oz / 150g fillets of monkfish
a little Dijon mustard
a little flour
a knob of butter
a little light olive oil
salt and freshly ground white pepper
To serve:
4 slices of smoked streaky bacon

First prepare the sauce: Put the shallots and mushrooms into a pan with the olive oil and cook gently until the onions are transparent. Add all the other ingredients, except the cream, butter and seasoning, and bring to the boil. Simmer, uncovered, until the liquid is reduced by two-thirds. Add the cream and reduce by a third. Strain through a fine sieve and re-boil in a clean pan, with the butter and seasoning.

To prepare the champ: Cook the potatoes in boiling salted water until tender, then skin them and push through a sieve or mash well. Boil the cream in a thick-bottomed pan and add the spring onions. Leave for 30 seconds and follow with the potato, mixing to make a smooth purée. Stir in the butter with a wooden spoon and season well. Keep warm.

To prepare the celeriac: Boil the celeriac in milk and water until tender; drain and set aside. When required, reheat in the cream and Dijon mustard. Add the chopped chives as you take it off the heat; season to taste.

To cook the monkfish: Rub the monkfish fillets lightly with Dijon mustard and lightly roll in flour. Sauté in a little butter and olive oil and cook over a medium heat for 3-4 minutes on each side. Set aside to rest. Meanwhile, grill the smoked bacon until crispy

To assemble the dish: Place a quarter of the champ in the middle of each warmed plate and top with a monkfish fillet. Place cubes of celeriac at equal intervals around it, drizzle with red wine sauce and top with crispy smoked bacon.

Chocolate fondant

At Chapter One, these chocolate fondants are served restaurant-style with a crème brulée ravioli and an unusual basil ice cream as well as the warm sauce given. At home, serve this luscious hot dessert more simply with accompaniments of your choice, preferably including an ice cream, and the Chapter One Grand Marnier Sauce.

Serves 4
3 whole eggs
5oz / 150g / ⁵/₈ cup caster sugar
3oz / 75g / 5¹/₄ US tablespoons
  (when melted), best dark chocolate
  (70% cocoa solids),
4oz / 100g / 1 stick unsalted butter,
  melted and cooled
1¹/₂oz / 40g / ¹/₃ cup plain flour
Grand Marnier sauce:
Juice of 4 oranges
4fl oz / 100 ml / scant ¹/₂ cup Grand
  Marnier
1 vanilla pod, split and de-seeded
1oz / 30g / generous ¹/₈ cup caster
  sugar.

First, prepare the sauce: Place all ingredients in a pan over moderate heat, dissolve the sugar then simmer, uncovered, to reduce by one third.

Meanwhile, preheat a moderate oven, 350°F / 180°C / gas mark 4.

To prepare the chocolate fondants: Beat the eggs and sugar together until pale and creamy. Add the melted chocolate, the butter and the flour, and mix everything together. Take four chilled dariole moulds or ramekins and grease them thoroughly with softened butter, then dust lightly with flour. Pour the mixture into the moulds and bake in the preheated oven for 8 minutes. (The outside will be crisp and the centre still runny).

To serve: Upturn the moulds over the centre of four heated plates and allow the chocolate fondants to slide out. Place a generous scoop of ice cream of your choice alongside, and drizzle the orange sauce around them.

Martin Corbett

Coopershill House

Riverstown, Co Sligo

Standing at the centre of a 500 acre estate of deer farm and woodland, this sturdy granite mansion has been home to seven generations of the O'Hara family since 1774, and was built to withstand the rigours of a Sligo winter. Neat rows of chimneys crown the perfectly maintained slate roof, hinting at the warmth to be found within the stern grey walls of one of Ireland's most delightful and superbly comfortable Georgian houses. Nothing about this immaculate house escapes Brian O'Hara's disciplined proprietorial eye and not only has the original eighteenth century furniture survived, but also some fascinating features - notably a Victorian bath complete with fully integrated cast-iron shower 'cubicle', in full working order, and a 'copper' once used for boiling the household's linen in the old basement laundry. Lindy runs the house and kitchen with the seamless hospitality born of long experience and log fires, candlelight and a wide choice of wines enhance her deliciously unpretentious food, served in their lovely dining room where the family silver is used with magnificent insouciance, even at breakfast.

Pot roast venison in red wine

The O'Haras farm venison at Coopershill, so guests often have the opportunity to enjoy this tender, lean meat from young animals under two years old. This tasty pot roast is one of Lindy's favourite recipes, and is ideal for gentle cooking in the Aga; it is also suitable for wild venison.

Serves 6-8

1 leg venison (farmed or wild), about 4lb / 2kg
2oz / 60g / 4 US tablespoons vegetable oil
2 onions, sliced
1 small turnip, chopped
8oz / 225g / 2 cups carrots, chopped
bouquet garni
6 juniper berries
8oz / 225 ml / 1 cup good stock, either beef or chicken
Juice of a lemon
1 tbsp brown sugar
1 tbsp tomato purée

For the sauce:

1-2 tsp arrowroot, or cornflour, slaked in a little water
1 tbsp / 1¼ US tablespoons redcurrant jelly
4fl oz / 125ml / ½ cup full-bodied red wine

Preheat a moderate oven, 300°F / 150°C / gas mark 2

Heat a little oil in a flameproof casserole and brown the venison all over in it. Remove and set aside while making a bed of the onions, chopped root vegetables, bouquet garni and juniper berries, then replace the joint on top. Mix the stock with the lemon, brown sugar, and tomato purée and use as much as is needed to half cover the joint. Cover securely and cook slowly in the oven. If it is farmed venison allow 20 minutes to the lb/450g, and 20 minutes over for medium cooked, or 10 minutes to the lb/450g plus 10 minutes over for pinker meat. Wild venison, unless very young, may need to be cooked for 30 minutes to the lb/450g.

When cooked to your liking, drain off the pan juices, cover the venison and keep it warm. Blend a little of the hot liquid into the arrowroot then add to the rest of the pan juices, along with the redcurrant jelly and the wine, and bring to the boil. Simmer for about 10 minutes, until the sauce clears and thickens. Carve the joint and serve with braised red cabbage, green beans and roast or mashed potatoes.

Vanilla & ginger ice cream

This unusual ice cream is too thick to make in an ice-cream machine, so it is simply frozen in a freezer. At Coopershill it is normally served with sliced peaches, strawberries or another seasonal fruit, but any sort of fancy biscuit is also good.

Serves 6-8

4 eggs, separated
3 or 4 drops vanilla extract
3oz / 75g (about 6 pieces) stem
  ginger in syrup
10fl oz / 300ml / 1¹/₃ cups double
  cream
6oz / 170g / 1¹/₃ cups icing sugar,
  sifted

Lightly beat the egg yolks and vanilla. Chop the ginger. Whip the cream until soft peaks form. Whisk the egg whites until firm peaks form and then gradually whisk in the icing sugar. Fold the egg yolks, ginger and cream into the meringue mixture. Pour into a freezer-proof container and freeze for at least six hours before serving.

Cromleach Lodge

Castlebaldwin, Co Sligo

Few views could rival the beauty of Lough Arrow seen from the restaurant at Cromleach, a modern lodge built by Christy and Moira Tiqhe to take full advantaqe of its quiet hillside position - and to ensure a fair share of the view for every diner from its thoughtfully arranged series of dining rooms. Lovely simple table settings - crisp linen, modern silver and crystal, and fine, understated china - provide a fit background for dinner, the high point of every visit to Cromleach: thanks to Moira's skilful handling of carefully sourced local ingredients, a meal here is always memorable. Daily-changed menus include a selection from an ever-growing range of specialities alongside newer dishes and, from the appetisers served with aperitifs in the bar to the irresistible plate of petits fours that round off the evening, details are invariably superb. Christy and Moira spare no effort to ensure comfort, relaxation and privacy for their guests, making a stay here exceptionally restorative; genuine hospitality shows in the smallest gestures - your exceptionally spacious bedroom will contain a jug of fresh milk in the fridge for your tea and coffee, for example - and every aspect of the housekeeping is outstanding.

White & dark chocolate mousse gateau

This rich dessert would make a dramatic finale for a dinner party. At Cromleach it is accompanied by fresh raspberries and crème anglaise, or it can be served simply with whipped cream flavoured with a little Baileys Irish Cream.

Serves 12
For the chocolate mousse:
6oz / 175g best dark chocolate
2 eggs, separated
15fl oz / 450ml / 2 cups cream
1fl oz / 25ml / 2 US tablespoons Tia Maria
6oz / 175g white chocolate
4 leaves gelatine (1oz / 25g if using powdered gelatine)
1fl oz / 25ml / 2 US tablespoons Baileys Irish Cream
2fl oz / 50ml / 4 US tablespoons Irel chicory and coffee with added sugar, or strong expresso with 1 tsp sugar.

For the nougatine topping:
The juice of half a lemon
1 tablespoon / 1¹/₂ US tablespoons golden syrup
4oz / 100g / ¹/₂ cup caster sugar
4oz / 100g / 1 cup nibbed (chopped) almonds

For the Baileys crème anglaise:
10fl oz / 300ml / 1¹/₃ cup cream
2 vanilla pods
2 egg yolks
3oz / 75g / ¹/₃ cup caster sugar
1fl oz / 25ml / 2 US tablespoons Baileys Irish Cream

Butter a loose-based round tin 9 in / 23cm x 1³/₄ inch / 4.5 cm deep, and line the sides with parchment paper.

First make the nougatine: Put the lemon juice, golden syrup, and sugar in a heavy based saucepan over a medium heat until the mixture turns golden brown. Add the almonds and stir vigorously until the mixture crumbles. Spread this mixture on greaseproof paper and allow to cool completely. Place on a clean dry tea-towel and using a rolling pin crush until you have a fine crumbed texture. Store in an airtight container.

To make the gateau: Soak the gelatine in a little cold water to soften. If using leaf, remove the gelatine from the water when soft and squeeze gently to remove excess liquid. Break the chocolates into small pieces and melt in two separate bowls set over hot (but not boiling) water. Add 1 egg yolk to each bowl, stir and remove the bowls from the heat. Warm the Baileys, add half of the gelatine (2 leaves, or ¹/₂oz / 12.5g if powered) and dissolve over a gentle heat; stir into the white chocolate mixture. Warm the Tia Maria, add the remaining gelatine and dissolve over a gentle heat; stir this into the dark chocolate mixture. Lightly whip the cream in one bowl and, in another, lightly whisk the egg whites. Gently fold half of the cream and half of the egg whites into each chocolate mixture. Add the coffee to the dark chocolate mixture only. Sprinkle a layer of the nougatine mixture on the base of the tin. Pour the dark chocolate mousse into the tin. Sprinkle with a layer of nougatine. Place in the freezer until set (about 15 minutes). Pour the white chocolate mixture over the set dark mousse, finishing with a thin layer of nougatine, and place in the fridge to set.

Crème anglaise: Put the cream and vanilla pod into a saucepan; bring to the boil and simmer gently for 8-10 minutes to infuse. Meanwhile whisk the egg yolks and caster sugar together until pale and creamy. Strain the cream over the egg mixture and mix well. Return to the rinsed saucepan and simmer over low heat, stirring, until a coating consistency is reached (do not boil). Strain and cool. Add Baileys to taste.

To serve: Remove the gateau from the tin. Using a sharp knife dipped in hot water, cut into wedges. Serve with the Crème Anglaise, and fresh seasonal fruit.

Smoked haddock tartlet

At Cromleach Lodge, Moira uses un-dyed oak-smoked haddock from Sally Barnes, Woodcock Smokery in West Cork for this pretty starter. For an simpler variation, the filling could be cooked in shallow china ramekins instead.

Serves 6

10fl oz / 300 ml / 1⅓ cups milk
10fl oz / 300 ml / 1⅓ cups cream
4 scallions (spring onions), chopped
18oz / 500g smoked haddock fillets
1oz / 25g / 2 tablespoons butter
1oz / 25g / 1½ US tablespoons white flour
½ tbsp Dijon mustard
1 egg yolk
2oz / 50g / ½ cup white cheddar cheese, grated
6 x 3½ inch / 9 cm prepared tartlet cases, or ramekins
Salt and freshly ground pepper

Preheat a moderate oven, 350°F / 180°C / gas mark 4

In a saucepan, bring the milk and cream to the boil over moderate heat, then add the onions and smoked haddock and cook over very low heat (not even simmering) for six minutes. In a separate pan, mix the butter and flour together to make a roux and cook gently over a low heat until it crumbles. Strain the liquid from the haddock, taking care not to break up the fish. Slowly add enough haddock liquid to the roux to make a thick white sauce. If it is too thick, adjust the consistency with a little water. Simmer the sauce for 10 minutes on a low heat, stirring continuously. Stir in the mustard and season with salt and freshly ground pepper.

Flake the haddock and gently mix with the sauce and spring onions; stir until the fish is well coated with the sauce, then gently blend in half the cheese and the egg yolk. Divide the mixture between the tartlets or ramekins, filling them about half full. Sprinkle the remainder of the cheese on top. Bake for 10-12 minutes or until golden brown.

Currarevagh House

Oughterard, Co Galway

Hospitality runs deep at Currarevagh, an early Victorian manor set in 150 acres of woodlands and gardens and run as a relaxed country house by Harry and June Hodgson, and their son Henry. It was built by their ancestors in 1842 and, when people talk about "going back to the style of an earlier era", this is the kind of place they have in mind. Tranquillity, trout and tea in the drawing room are the things that draw guests back time and again to this house where the atmosphere is more like a private house party than an hotel. The restful rituals that form part of the everyday routine at Currarevagh underline the differences: a breakfast worthy of its Edwardian origins, a picnic hamper for lunch, then afternoon tea, to be followed by a leisurely dinner, all based on fresh local produce. Fishing is the ruling passion, of course - notably brown trout, pike, perch and salmon - but there are plenty of other pursuits to assist in building up an appetite for June's unpretentious home cooking.

Connemara lamb marinated in port and honey, with a tomato & mint chutney

Connemara is renowned for its lamb and Currarevagh is supplied by Finnerty's butchers in Oughterard, where Gerry Conneely provides racks with very little fat on them. One full rack should be sufficient for nine people, so this recipe can be adapted accordingly. Get your butcher to bone the rack for you so that the marinade will permeate the meat easily. The minted chutney is an unusual alternative to traditional mint sauce as an accompaniment.

Serves 9
1 full rack of lamb (weight before
    boning about 5.5lb / 2.5kg), boned

Marinade:
7fl oz / 200ml / 1 cup soy sauce
7fl oz / 200ml / 1 cup port
7fl oz / 200ml / $^3/_4$ cup honey
5fl oz / 150ml / $^2/_3$ cup fresh orange
    juice
1 tbsp / 1$^1/_4$ US tablespoons balsamic
    vinegar
1 sprig rosemary
salt and freshly ground black pepper
    to taste

Tomato and mint chutney:
15fl oz / 450ml / 2 cups brown sugar
15fl oz / 450ml / 2 cups red wine
    vinegar
2 x 14oz / 400g tins of plum
    tomatoes
2 bay leaves
1 bunch fresh mint, chopped

First make the chutney: Place all the ingredients, except the mint, in a saucepan. Bring to the boil slowly, stirring to dissolve the sugar, then reduce the heat and simmer very gently for about one hour or until it has reduced in volume by at least half. Remove bay leaves, stir in the mint and season to taste. This is best served hot, although it is also good cold.

To prepare the lamb: Mix the marinade ingredients and marinate the lamb in the fridge overnight.

Preheat a very hot oven, 425°F / 220°C / gas mark 7.

Meanwhile, roll the meat neatly and tie with string at 1 in/ 3cm intervals and then cut in half, to ensure even cooking. Place the meat in a large roasting tin and pour the marinade over it. Roast for 20 minutes and then leave to rest for a further 20 minutes or until you are ready to slice it. The meat will be tender and pink so, if it is preferred medium to well done, it should be left it in the oven for a further 10–20 minutes. Slice and serve with seasonal vegetables and the Tomato and Mint Chutney.

Baked lemon sponge

This lovely old-fashioned pudding is typical of the wholesome good food served at Currarevagh. It is usually served hot, but is also delicious cold - although it may look as if the centre has sunk a little when cold.

Serves 6-8
4oz / 110g / 1 stick plus 1 US
*   tablespoon butter*
7oz / 200g / 2 cups granulated sugar
4 medium eggs, separated
4oz / 110g / 1 cup plain white flour
grated rind and juice of 2 lemons
1¹/₂ pints / 900 ml / 4 cups milk
To serve:
caster sugar and whipped cream

Preheat a moderate oven, 350°F / 180°C / Gas 4.

Using an electric mixer, cream the butter and sugar until light and fluffy. Gradually add in the yolks of eggs, and then the flour; beating all the time; add the grated lemons and juice. Incorporate the milk slowly, stopping the mixer half way through in order to scrape the mixture down the sides of the mixing bowl. Don't worry if it appears slightly curdled. Whisk the egg whites separately until they form soft peaks, then fold into the mixture.

Butter a 3 pint / 1.75 litre pie dish and pour the mixture into it. Place the dish in a roasting tin and add hot water to come about ³/₄ inch / 2 cm up the sides of the tin.

Bake for 45 minutes, or until the top is golden brown and the pudding feels fairly firm to the touch. If necessary, reduce the heat and bake for a further 15 minutes. Underneath the sponge there should be a deliciously lemony custard. Serve hot, sprinkled with caster sugar, and offer whipped cream on the side.

Doyle's

Dingle, Co Kerry

Originally a small pub built in 1790, Doyles was established as a restaurant over a quarter of a century ago - and was one of the first in a town which is now renowned for good eating places. Currently run by Sean Cluskey and his wife Charlotte, it's a cosy, characterful place with an old kitchen range and natural materials - stone floor, kitchen tables and sugan chairs, a real wooden bar and high stools - that all create a relaxed country atmosphere in keeping with its history. Local seafood is the main attraction - nightly specials depend on the day's landings - and lobster, selected from a tank in the bar, is a speciality. There are, however, one or two concessions to non-seafood eaters such as Kerry mountain lamb done various ways (roast rack and leg with braised puy lentils, roast garlic & thyme jus is a favourite) or traditional beef & Guinness stew. Accommodation is also offered, in eight spacious and recently refurbished bedrooms with well-designed en-suite bathrooms, and there's a comfortable residents' sitting room as well.

Seared scallops, baby spinach and crispy bacon, with balsamic dressing

The combination of fresh scallops with bacon wakens the taste buds, and the sweetness of the dressing brings this attractive dish together.

Serves 4
12 medium-sized scallops, cleaned
*   and trimmed*
12 thin slices streaky bacon
9oz / 250g / 4 cups baby spinach
*   leaves, washed and dried.*
1 tbsp olive oil
Dressing:
5fl oz / 150 ml / ³/₄ cup balsamic
*   vinegar*
1 tsp honey
1 tbsp / 1¹/₄ US tablespoons red wine
5floz / 150 ml / ³/₄ cup olive oil

First make the dressing: Place the balsamic vinegar, honey and red wine in a saucepan. Bring to boiling point, then reduce the heat and simmer for about 10 minutes or until reduced in volume by half. Chill, and then blend in the olive oil. The dressing should be the consistency of honey and, when drizzled in a ring around the plate, be thick enough to enclose the juices. Any surplus dressing will keep well, covered, for about 2 weeks in the fridge.

To cook the dish: Grill the bacon until crisp. Meanwhile heat the olive oil in a large frying pan. Season the scallops, then sear for 1-2 minutes without moving them. Turn and sear on other side for 1 minute. Take care not to overcook them or they will become tough.

To serve: Mix the spinach with two tablespoons of the dressing to make a salad and arrange in the centre of each warmed plate; place the bacon on top, then arrange three of the scallops around the edge of the leaves, and drizzle a little more dressing around the edge of the plate.

Spiced spotted dick with egg custard

Steamed suet puddings bring back happy memories of school dinners for many people. This version gets a lift with lemon zest and spice, and the real egg custard is delicious.

Serves 6

3oz / 75g / ¹/₃ cup soft white flour
3oz / 75g / ¹/₃ cup strong white flour
a scant 2 tbsp / 25g / 2¹/₂ scant US tablespoons baking powder
3oz / 75g grated suet
5fl oz / 150ml / ²/₃ cup water
1 tsp mixed spice
6oz / 175g / 1 cup plus 1 US tablespoon sultanas
a pinch salt
a little butter, softened
zest of one lemon

Egg custard:

10fl oz / 300ml / 1¹/₃ cups milk
2 egg yolks
1oz / 25g / 1¹/₄ US tablespoons caster sugar
2-3 drops vanilla essence

First prepare the moulds: Everyday teacups or small bowls are fine (6 x ¼ pint / 150ml). Rub the inside of each mould with butter and dust with a little flour.

To make the puddings: Place all the ingredients except the water in a mixing bowl. Mix lightly by hand. Add the water and mix lightly again. Fill each individual mould three-quarters full with the mixture. Cover with greaseproof paper and then cover with foil. Tie tightly with string to prevent water getting into the puddings while they boil. Place in a steamer. Cover and steam for 45 minutes. (If cooking bain marie-style in the oven, hot water should come half way up the sides of the moulds.) When cooked, remove from the steamer or bain marie and stand for 10 minutes before turning the puddings out of the moulds.

To make the custard: Put the milk in a saucepan and bring up to boiling point. Whisk the egg yolks, sugar and vanilla essence together to make a creamy mixture, then gradually add the boiled milk, whisking constantly. Pour the mixture into the rinsed saucepan and place over a very gentle heat. Cook, stirring with a wooden spoon, until the mixture is thick enough to coat the back of the spoon. Do not allow to boil, or the eggs will scramble.

To serve: Turn the hot puddings onto warmed plates and pour a little custard over the top.

Dunbrody House

Arthurstown, Co Wexford

Set in twenty acres of parkland and gardens, Kevin and Catherine Dundon's magnificent Georgian manor has access to Duncannon beach - where the herons that inspired their emblem are plentiful along the foreshore. The house has been elegantly restored to enhance its gracious proportions, and includes an extension which was painstakingly built to match the original house in every detail; the large bedrooms - which include suites and state rooms - have fine views to match the opulent furnishings, and lofty reception rooms include The Harvest Room restaurant, with elegantly draped windows overlooking the terrace and a log fire adding comfort and atmosphere in winter. Catherine tends front of house with style and warmth, while Kevin is renowned for his support of local produce and leads a fine kitchen team, cooking in a unique contemporary style that also acknowledges tradition. A productive organic vegetable and fruit garden supplies the kitchen all year round - a special point of interest to students at the stylish cookery school the Dundons have created in restored outbuildings, and for guests at the Dunbrody Spa who enjoy exciting new energising menus based on freshly-picked produce in season.

Garden cherry tomatoes and olive linguini

Although local meats - and a great deal of local seafood - feature regularly on Dunbrody House menus, vegetarian dishes are also a strong point, often using produce just picked from their own kitchen garden.

Serves 4
14oz / 400g fresh linguini - egg or spinach
olive oil
1 medium sized onion, finely sliced
2 cloves garlic, finely chopped
3^1/$_2$oz / 100g / ^{1}/$_2$ cup cherry tomatoes, halved
3^1/$_2$oz / 100g / ^{3}/$_4$ cup black olives, pitted
4fl oz / 100ml / ^{1}/$_2$ cup dry white wine
2oz / 50g / 1^1/$_2$ cups parsley, roughly chopped
sea salt
cracked black pepper
4oz / 120g / ^{3}/$_4$ cup Parmesan shavings

Bring a large pan of water to the boil with a dash of olive oil and a pinch of salt; add the linguini and cook on a high heat for 7 minutes, then drain.

Set a large frying pan over a high heat, add a dash of olive oil and then the onions and garlic; cook for about 4 minutes, until golden brown. Add the cherry tomatoes and black olives. Next add the white wine and chopped parsley, and season to taste with sea salt and black pepper. Remove from the heat and add the linguini; place in four pasta bowls and place the parmesan shavings on top.

Strawberry temptation

Simple can be best, even in the finest hotels - as this delicious way with strawberries from the Dunbrody kitchen garden shows.

Serves 4
3¹/₂oz / 100g / ¹/₂ cup mascarpone cheese
1oz / 30g / 2 scant US tablespoons caster sugar
4fl oz / 100ml / ¹/₂ cup double cream, whipped
2floz / 50ml / ¹/₄ cup Grand Marnier
14oz / 400g strawberries, halved
2¹/₂oz / 60g / 4 US tablespoons brown sugar

Mix the marscarpone cheese and sugar together in a bowl until it forms a creamy texture; fold in the whipped cream and Grand Marnier. Divide this mixture between four espresso coffee cups or dessert glasses. Place each cup on a plate and arrange the strawberries around. Sprinkle the brown sugar over the top of the cream and the strawberries. To eat, you dip the strawberries into the cream - yum!

Dunbrody soufflé of Abbey Blue cheese, with a watercress salad

A classic soufflé is given a new twist with locally produced farmhouse cheese and contemporary presentation.

Serves 4

2oz / 50g / ¹/₂ cup brioche crumbs or
 breadcrumbs
1¹/₂oz / 40g / ¹/₃ cup ground walnuts

For the soufflés:

2oz / 50g / ¹/₂ stick butter, softened
2oz / 50g / ¹/₃ cup plain flour
5fl oz / 150ml / ³/₄ cup milk
2 egg yolks
3¹/₂oz / 100g / scant cup Abbey Blue
 cheese, crumbled
salt and freshly ground pepper
5 egg whites
a few drops lemon juice
7oz / 200g / 3 cups (a good bunch)
 watercress

First prepare the moulds: Butter 4 cappuccino cups with soft butter. Mix the brioche crumb and walnuts, and use to coat the cups, then freeze. Repeat this process three times in order to obtain a good coating.

Preheat a hot oven, 425°F / 210°C / gas mark 7.

To make the soufflés: Melt the butter in a saucepan and slowly add the flour, stirring constantly until the mixture becomes a light-coloured roux. Gradually mix in the milk to make a thick béchamel and stir in the 2 egg yolks. Add the Abbey Blue and blend lightly. Put this mixture into a mixing bowl and season with salt and pepper. Whisk the egg whites to a firm peak. Stir in a tablespoonful of the egg white to loosen the mixture then, using a metal spoon, lightly fold in the remaining egg whites. Divide the mixture between the four prepared cups and bake in the preheated oven for 15 minutes, or until the soufflés are well-risen and golden brown but still a little wobbly in the centre.

To serve: Put the soufflés, in their cups, onto four serving plates, with the watercress salad on the side of the plate - dress simply with a squeeze of lemon juice and some cracked black pepper.

◄ Kevin Dundon
 Proprietor-chef,
 Dunbrody House & Cookery School

Enniscoe House

Ballina, Co Mayo

"The last great house of North Mayo" was built by ancestors of the present owner, Susan Kellett, who settled here in the 1660s, and is a very special place for anglers and visitors with a natural empathy for the untamed wildness of the area. Set in parkland and mature woods on the shores of Lough Conn, the house may sometimes seem stern and gaunt, as Georgian mansions in the north-west of Ireland tend to be, but any intimidating impressions are quickly dispelled once inside. The house has great charm and makes a lovely place to come back to after a day in the rugged countryside - family portraits, antique furniture and crackling log fires all complement Susan's warm hospitality and good home cooking. And there is also much of interest around converted outbuildings at the back of the house, including a genealogy centre, a small but expanding agricultural museum with working blacksmith, self-catering accommodation, conference facilities - and a walled garden under restoration, with an informal restaurant overlooking it, an exquisite little gift shop, and an extensive organic kitchen garden that supplies vegetables to the house.

Almond tea biscuits

These biscuits are very sweet, and are usually served with sharp fruit like rhubarb or gooseberry fool as a dessert, rather than at tea time.

Makes 12
2 eggs
3oz / 75g / ¹/₃ cup caster sugar
finely grated rind of 1 lemon
¹/₂ tsp ground cinnamon
a few drops almond essence
2oz / 50g / ¹/₂ cup plain flour
3oz / 75g / ²/₃ cup ground almonds
1oz / 25g / ¹/₄ cup almonds, flaked
a little butter

Preheat a moderate oven, 350°F / 180°C / gas mark 4.

Beat the eggs and sugar together until light and fluffy. Add the grated lemon rind, cinnamon, and a few drops of almond essence. Sift the flour, mix with the ground almonds, then fold into the egg mixture and blend well. Butter twelve small flat tart tins and dust with flour. Divide the mixture between the tins, top with flaked almonds and bake in the preheated oven for 15 minutes. Remove from the tins while still hot and cool on a rack. Patty tins may be used for baking instead, and the end result will look more like a tea cake but will taste just as good.

Roast loin of pork
with apricot & walnut sauce

There is an organic farm near Ennsicoe, and the pork supplied is exceptional. The slight sweetness of the apricots and the crunch of the walnuts goes well with this delicious meat, and a really crisp crackling is the pièce de résistance. For this, get the butcher to score the skin and remove it from the joint, to cook separately.

Serves 6
*loin of pork (about 1.3 kg / 3 lb
   weight)*
a little olive oil
a little salt
Sauce:
*4oz / 110g / $^3/_4$ cup dried apricots,
   chopped in half*
*10fl oz / 300ml / 1$^1/_3$ cups dry white
   wine*
1 medium onion, finely chopped
*4$^1/_2$oz / 140g / 1$^1/_2$ sticks cold butter,
   diced*
parsley to garnish
*2oz / 50g / $^1/_3$ cup walnuts, roughly
   chopped*

Ahead of cooking, put the apricots in the white wine and soak for at least 4 hours (or overnight).

Preheat a fairly hot oven, 375°F / 190°C / gas mark 5.

Place the pork in a roasting tin. Rub the skin with the olive oil and salt, and lay on top of the joint. Roast in the preheated oven for about two hours, removing the skin after one and a half hours (if the skin is not crisp by then continue to roast it, but separately from the joint). The pork is cooked when the juices run clear.

To make the sauce: Drain the soaked apricots and set aside; put the wine into a pan with the onion, bring up to the boil and simmer until the volume is reduced to 2 tablespoons. Beat in the butter, bit by bit (this works best if the butter is really cold). Add the reserved apricots and the walnuts, and stir in well. Keep the sauce just warm until ready to serve.

To serve: Carve off slices of pork, allowing two good slices per person. Arrange on warmed plates, with a spoonful of sauce over one slice, and some pieces of the pork skin crackling. Sprinkle with chopped parsley and serve.

St Ernans House Hotel
Donegal, Co Donegal

Quietly situated on a private wooded tidal island, approached by a causeway built after the famine by tenants as a gesture of gratitude to a caring landlord, Brian and Carmel O'Dowd's lovely Victorian house on the edge of Donegal town owes its special atmosphere to a unique location - but also, one imagines, to the kindly ghosts who seem to reside here, notably the spirit of John Hamilton, that young landlord who built the house in 1826. The other-worldliness of St Ernans remains, a timeless serenity that is almost tangible on ascending the unusual entrance steps, lined with pot plants and still protected by their original Victorian glazing. It's the perfect place to find deep restfulness: in the quietness of your room, close your eyes and listen - the elements will seem very close as you hear the water sluicing or gently trickling by, the wind in the trees, birdsong perhaps...In wilder weather it's a safe haven, somewhere to relax beside the fire and respond to gentle hospitality, knowing that the salmon you are offered for dinner will have been caught within sight of your bedroom window.

Fresh tomato & basil soup

A delicious soup best made in the summer when tomatoes are most flavoursome and in plentiful supply, and when basil is at its leafy best. This soup, full of summer flavours, needs no accompaniment other than some fresh crusty home-made bread. For a creamier, more delicate, soup fresh cream may be added.

Serves 4-6
1oz / 25g / 2 US tablespoons butter
1oz / 25g bacon trimmings
2oz / 50g / ⅓ cup carrot, chopped
2oz / 50g / ½ cup leek, chopped
2oz / 50g / ½ cup onion chopped
*1oz / 25g / 2 US tablespoons tomato
  purée*
*2 lb / 900g / 4 cups fresh tomatoes,
  roughly chopped*
*2 pints / 1.2 litres / 1 quart chicken or
  vegetable stock*
fresh basil leaves

Melt the butter in a heavy saucepan and add the bacon, carrot, leek and onion. Cover and cook for about 10 minutes, or until the vegetables are cooked but not coloured. Add the tomato purée and the roughly chopped tomatoes and cook on a low heat for a further 10 minutes. Add the stock, bring to the boil, then simmer for 30 minutes. Liquidise the soup and strain it to remove the tomato skins and seeds. Season with salt and freshly ground black pepper and add a good bunch of roughly chopped basil leaves. Serve hot.

Warm smoked salmon on a potato cake with sour cream & chives

Warming the smoked salmon gives this popular starter a more subtle flavour, that is then complemented by the sour cream delicately scented with fresh chives. The potato cake forms a perfect base to make this an all-round superb dish.

Serves 4

1 lb / 450g potatoes (2 cups when mashed)
2oz / 50g / ½ stick butter
2oz / 50g / ½ cup flour
salt and freshly ground pepper
12oz / 325g smoked salmon, trimmed and thinly sliced
a little sour cream
fresh chives, finely chopped

Peel, boil and drain the potatoes, then mash with the butter until very smooth. Add the flour and salt and pepper and mix together. Knead lightly and roll out to a thickness of about ½ inch / 1.2 cm. Cut into large circles 3-4 inches / 7.5-10 cm in diameter. Cook on a heavy pan for 2 to 3 minutes each side until golden brown.

Place a potato cake on each of four warm plates and arrange the smoked salmon on top. Place the plates under a hot grill until the smoked salmon is just warmed. Mix the finely chopped chives with the sour cream and put a spoonful on top of the warm salmon. Serve immediately.

Glassdrumman Lodge

Annalong, Co Down

In the heart of the ancient 'Kingdom of Mourne', Glassdrumman Lodge is in a dramatic hillside location just outside the village of Annalong on the County Down coast, and close to the great forest parks of Tollymore and Castlewellan. The lodge has been developed by the present owners, Graeme and Joan Hall, from what was once a typical Mourne farmhouse into an unusual country house, where fresh produce comes from their own gardens, and local seafood from nearby ports. Nestling between the magnificent Mountains of Mourne and the surging east coast seas, in an area

where you could be forgiven for thinking that they 'grow' the boulders for dry stone walls, Glassdrumman is not only scenically located in one of Ireland's most picturesque mountain districts, but also perfectly placed for golfers who wish to play the world famous County Down Golf Course - and for fishing folk, who may prefer casting for trout on the well-stocked lake to other more energetic outdoor activities like walking and climbing.

Mediterranean scallops

Local scallops get the sunshine treatment in this colourful starter or light main dish.

Serves 4
4 medium vine-ripened tomatoes
3 cloves garlic, finely chopped
1/8 pint / 75 ml / 1/4 cup virgin olive oil
1/4 pint / 150ml / 1/2 cup balsamic
    vinegar
salt, freshly ground pepper & a little
    sugar
12 king scallops, shelled
1 Vienna loaf

Slice the tomatoes and put into a bowl with the garlic, olive oil, balsamic vinegar and a light seasoning of salt, pepper and sugar. Trim the scallops, slice in half crossways and drain well on a wooden board. Lightly oil four 3/4 inch / 2 cm thick slices of bread and brown on a griddle or under the grill to make four thick croûtes. Heat the griddle again until very hot, lightly oil it and grill the scallops for 1-2 minutes, turning once.

To serve: Lay the croûtes on four warmed plates. Remove the tomatoes from the marinade and lay them on top, then arrange the scallops on top of the tomatoes, with their corals to the side, and drizzle the marinade over the top. Garnish with a sprig of fennel and serve immediately.

Oven-roast fillet of beef
with red wine & garlic sauce

Pride is taken in the quality of beef used at Glasdrumman, and this is a favourite dish.

Serves 8
4 lb / 2 kg dry aged beef fillet
* (trimmed)*
¹/₂ bottle of red wine
2 bulbs of garlic
6 tips of fresh rosemary, or thyme
8oz / 225g / 2¹/₄ sticks butter
salt, freshly ground black pepper &
* olive oil.*

Preheat a very hot oven, 450°F / 230°C / gas mark 8.

Brush the beef with olive oil, then season with salt and a grinding of pepper.

Heat a dry frying pan until very hot, then seal the beef in it, just colouring the meat the whole way around.

Peel all the garlic and, leaving the cloves whole, put them in the base of a deep casserole dish. Lay the beef on top of the garlic cloves and sprinkle the roughly chopped herb on top. Roast the beef in the preheated oven for 20 minutes, then remove from the oven, add the wine to the dish and lay the butter on top of the meat.

Roast for a further 20 minutes, turning as necessary. Turn the oven down to 350°F / 180°C / gas mark 4 for a further 20 minutes, then remove the meat from the dish and let it rest for in a warm place for15 minutes.

Reserve any juices that come out of the resting meat and add to the wine, butter and juices from the casserole. Remove the garlic if you wish, or push through a sieve to blend it with the sauce. Boil the juices to reduce to a sauce consistency; slice the beef as thickly or thinly as you wish, and serve with the red wine and garlic sauce.

Apple pie

Everyone's favourite comfort food to round off a wholesome meal - this is the Glassdrumman version of traditional apple pie.

Serves 8
Pastry:
6oz / 175g / ³/₄ cup caster sugar
12oz / 350g / 3¹/₂ sticks butter
1 lb / 450g / 4 cups (firmly packed) plain flour
Filling:
6oz / 175g / ³/₄ cup granulated sugar, approx.
12oz / 350g approx. peeled, cored & sliced Bramley apples (prepared weight)

Cream the butter and sugar until soft, then gradually blend in the flour and mix everything together to make a firm but pliable pastry. Leave in the fridge to rest for half an hour.

Preheat a fairly hot oven 400°F / 200°C / gas mark 6.

Roll out half of the pastry on a floured board to about ¼ inch / ½ cm thickness and use to cover an ovenproof dinner plate of about 9½ inch / 24cm diameter. Slice off the excess from around the edge. Put the sliced apple in the centre of the plate in a heap about 4 inch / 10 cm high, and leave about 1 inch / 3 cm around the edge of the plate, then sprinkle the sugar over the top of the apple. Dampen the pastry all around the edge. Roll out the remaining pastry, slightly thicker than before, and completely cover the apple and the plate. Gently shape the crust around the apple to make a 1 inch / 3 cm crust around the edge of the plate. Trim off the excess pastry and seal the edge of the pie by gently pressing the pastry down with your thumb at about ½ inch / 1 cm intervals. Trim the excess pastry once more and prick the top of the pie several times with a knife. Bake the pie in the preheated oven for 30-45 minutes, or until the pastry is a nice golden straw colour.

Serve warm, with chilled pouring cream, whipped cream or vanilla ice cream.

Glin Castle

Glin, Co Limerick

Surrounded by formal gardens and parkland, Glin Castle stands proudly on the south bank of the Shannon; the FitzGeralds, hereditary Knights of Glin, have lived here for 700 years and it is now the home of the 29th Knight and his wife Madame FitzGerald. The interior is stunning, with beautiful rooms enhanced by decorative plasterwork and magnificent collections of Irish furniture and paintings. But its most attractive feature is that everything is kept just the same as usual for guests, who are magnificently looked after by manager Bob Duff. Sensitive conversion has created lovely accommodation in rooms which all have the modern comforts, plus that indefinable atmosphere created by beautiful old things - when the Knight is at home he will take visitors on a tour of the house and show them all his pictures, furniture and other treasures. Interested guests will also relish the opportunity to enjoy the famous gardens, including the 2 acre walled kitchen gardens which provide an abundance of seasonal produce for the castle kitchens. The menu at Glin Castle changes daily with the seasons and as the head chef, Lionel, is Malaysian the menus also reflect his Asian talents, seen in varied menus with a hint of the exotic.

Desmond FitzGerald, the Knight of Glin

Peppered prime Irish beef fillet with chargrilled vegetables, champ and coffee barbecue sauce

Although the accompaniments may sometimes be exotic, this old favourite is basically one of the more traditional dishes at Glin Castle, and it can be presented as simply - or as fancifully - as you like.

Serves 4
4 x 6oz / 175g fillet steaks
freshly cracked black peppercorns
salt
2 tbsp olive oil

Champ:
3 lb / 1.4 kg large Irish floury potatoes
10-12fl oz / 300-350ml / 1^1/$_3$-1^1/$_2$ cups milk
4oz / 110g / 1 cup scallions (spring onions), chopped
2oz / 50g / ^{1}/$_2$ stick butter

Sauce:
2 tbsp olive oil
3 large onions, diced
3 garlic cloves, chopped
4oz / 110g tinned tomatoes
3^1/$_3$oz / 100g / ^{1}/$_2$ cup brown sugar
4^1/$_2$fl oz / 125ml / ^{1}/$_2$ cup cider vinegar
4^1/$_2$fl oz / 125ml / ^{1}/$_2$ cup strong coffee
1 tbsp / 1^1/$_4$ US tablespoons Worcestershire sauce

Vegetables:
a selection of parsnips, carrots, courgettes and peppers
a little olive oil for char-grilling

First make the champ: Boil the potatoes in their jackets; drain well and return to the pan. Cover with milk and bring slowly to the boil. Simmer for 3-4 minutes. Turn off the heat and leave to infuse. Drain, reserving the milk. Peel and mash the potatoes. While still hot, add the chopped scallions and the hot milk; beat in the butter and season.

To make the sauce: Heat the olive oil in a saucepan, over moderate heat; add the onions and garlic, and cook gently until soft but not coloured. Add the tomatoes, sugar, vinegar, coffee and Worcestershire sauce. Bring to the boil, and simmer gently for 15 minutes.

Vegetables: Peel and slice (or dice) a selection of vegetables, such as parsnips, carrots, courgettes, peppers, as available. Toss in enough olive oil to coat. Start by roasting in a very hot oven (450°F / 250°C / gas mark 8) until just tender and finish under the grill, until lightly charred.

To cook the steaks: Roll the steaks in cracked pepper and season with a little salt. Heat a heavy pan, oil lightly and seal the steaks; reduce the heat and cook until done to your liking.

To serve: Place the champ on the middle of the plate, the steak on the top and the sauce around and on top of the steak and garnish with the char-grilled vegetables.

Lemongrass infused crème caramel with rhubarb & lime granita

Asian influences in the kitchen are seen again, in this classical dish with a twist.

Serves 6

Granita:
1lb / 450g / 2 cups palm sugar, or
   caster sugar
1 pint / 600ml / 2³/₄ cups water
10fl oz / 300ml / 1¹/₃ cups rhubarb
   juice
10fl oz / 300ml / 1¹/₃ cups fresh lime
   juice

Crème caramel:
3 stalks lemon grass, finely minced
4oz / 110g / ¹/₂ cup palm sugar or
   caster sugar
4fl oz / 100ml / ¹/₂ cup water
8fl oz / 225ml / 1 cup milk
8fl oz / 225ml / 1 cup coconut milk
4 eggs
2oz / 50g / ¹/₄ cup golden caster
   sugar
¹/₂ tsp pure vanilla essence

First make the granita: Put the sugar and water into a pan and heat, stirring, until the sugar has dissolved, then the boil for 2 minutes. Cool. Mix the fruit juices and sugar syrup together, put into a container and freeze for a couple of hours (until just beginning to freeze at the edge) then whisk the frozen mixture to a liquid. Refreeze until it is ready.

To make the crème caramel: Put half of the minced lemongrass into a heavy bottomed saucepan, together with the sugar and water. Over a gentle heat, stir until all the sugar is dissolved, then boil over moderate heat until the mixture turns to a rich brown caramel. Dip the pan into a pan of cool water to prevent the caramel from cooking any further, then pour the caramel syrup into 6 ramekins, swirling it around so that it coats the sides a little as well as the bottom.

Preheat a warm oven, 170°C / 325°F / gas mark 3.

Now put the milk and coconut milk into a saucepan with the balance of the lemon grass. Stir and heat until it starts to bubble around the edge. Meanwhile, whisk the eggs in a mixing bowl with the caster sugar and vanilla essence. Remove the milk from the heat and pour it steadily over the egg mixture, whisking all the time. Divide the mixture between the ramekins, place in a roasting tin with boiling water coming just half way up the ramekins. Bake in the preheated oven for 40 minutes or until just cooked. Remove from the oven and allow to cool.

To serve: Run a knife around the edge of each ramekin and turn them out onto individual dessert plates. Lay a ball of granita on top of each crème caramel and surround with the sauce. Alternatively, you can simply serve the crème caramel on its own, perhaps decorated with caramelised lemongrass and a fresh strawberry.

Gregans Castle

Ballyvaughan, Co Clare

Echoing, perhaps, the apparent harshness of the surrounding Burren - a moonscape where mile upon mile of forbidding grey limestone serves only to highlight the delicate beauty and jaunty colours of the rare alpine and arctic flowers that flourish amongst the rocks in early summer - the deceptive and beguiling rock-fortress of Gregans Castle conceals an oasis of comfort. Here the Haden family and an outstandingly obliging staff welcome guests to the warmth and comfort within, a haven that contrasts wonderfully with both the stark lines and silver-grey stone of the castle, and its surrounding landscape. Local produce, notably seafood landed nearby, Burren lamb and County Clare cheeses star on menus which change with the seasons - and the restaurant provides a wonderful setting for memorable dinners: on fine evenings there can be a mesmerising play of light over the Burren, as the sun goes down over Galway Bay. Hospitality, good food and - especially - peace and quiet are the dominant themes and the otherwise luxurious rooms are deliberately left without the worldly interference of television.

Galway Bay seafood terrine en croûte

Gregans Castle is fortunate to have fresh fish on the doorstep, and the Garrihy family from Doolin have been supplying the kitchens here for three decades. This terrine baked in a pastry case is very popular with guests.

Serves 6

7oz / 200g skinned & boned white
  fish, e.g. turbot, cod, monkfish,
  chilled
1 egg
7fl oz / 200ml / 1 cup cream, chilled
3¹/₂oz / 100g cooked mussels and
  clams
3¹/₂oz / 100g tinned sardines, drained
2 tsp chopped dill
salt and black pepper
Pastry:
6oz / 175g / 1¹/₃ cups plain flour
3¹/₂oz / 100g / 1 stick butter
¹/₂oz / 10g / scant US tablespoon
  caster sugar
a pinch of salt
1 egg
2 tbsp / 30 ml / 2¹/₂ US tablespoons
  cold water

Preheat a slow oven, 300°F / 150°C / gas mark 2. Grease a 10 x 3¹/₄ x 2¹/₄ inch / 25 x 8.5 x 6cm terrine mould.

First make the pastry: In a food processor, mix the flour and butter at a low speed for two or three minutes. Add the sugar, salt and egg, and mix at low speed until just combined. Slowly add the water and as soon as the pastry come together, remove it from the processor. Wrap in cling-film and allow to rest for, preferably for 6-12 hours.

Filling: In a food processor, mix the white fish and egg at high speed for 30 seconds then, at low speed, pour the cream over the fish and egg mixture. When combined, transfer into a bowl. Add the remaining ingredients and season with salt and pepper. Chill.

To make the terrine: Roll out the pastry to line the terrine mould, bringing the pastry up to the top on all sides. Pour the chilled fish mixture into the terrine, and use the remaining pastry to make a lid. Fit tightly, pasting well to the top of the pastry, and brush with egg wash. Cook the terrine in the preheated oven for 1 hour, or until the core temperature reaches 72°c. Remove from the oven and leave to cool. Refrigerate for 24 hrs before serving sliced, with a small salad garnish.

Irish Mist mousse

This classic cold sweet is a favourite at Gregans Castle.

Serves 8
1 pint / 600ml / 2³/₄ cups milk
4 eggs, separated
3oz / 75g / ¹/₃ cup caster sugar
2 tbsp / 30g / 2¹/₂ US tablespoons
  powdered gelatine
3fl oz / 75ml / ¹/₃ cup warm water
3fl oz / 75ml / ¹/₃ cup Irish Mist
  liqueur
9fl oz / 250ml / 1 cup plus 2 US
  tablespoons cream, lightly whipped

Put the milk into a saucepan and bring to the boil. Blend the egg yolks and sugar well then add a little of the hot milk to the egg mixture; when combined, return to the rinsed saucepan. Stir this mixture over a low heat until it coats the back of the spoon, making a custard. Strain the custard into a bowl. Put the the warm water into a bowl and sprinkle the gelatine over it; leave to soak for a minute or two then stir to dissolve. Add the melted gelatine and the Irish Mist to the custard, and stir to distribute evenly. Leave to cool. When just beginning to set, fold in the whipped cream. Finally, whisk the egg whites to soft peaks and carefully fold into the mousse with a metal spoon. Divide between 8 glasses and leave in the fridge to set. Serve decorated with whipped cream, a dusting of cocoa powder and perhaps some toasted chopped hazelnuts or pecan halves.

Hunter's Hotel

Rathnew, Co Wicklow

Set in lovely gardens alongside the River Vartry, this delightfully rambling hotel is one of Ireland's oldest coaching inns, dating back to 1720 - and it has been in the same family ownership now for five generations. Together with her family and staff, the colourful Mrs Maureen Gelletlie takes pride in running the place on traditional lines, with old-fashioned comfort and food based on local and home-grown produce a priority - the emphasis is very much on 'old fashioned', and that's where its character lies. The gardens have magnificent herbaceous borders and lawns a-plenty, making the perfect setting for one of their famous summer afternoon teas, an aperitif or a post-prandial coffee - and the open fire and chintz-covered chairs in the bar have equal charm in winter. Comments made in the Visitors Book through the years depict the charms of the hotel most eloquently

- as, indeed, do travellers' reports: "The Stranger in Ireland" by John Carr Esq. (London, 1806), includes a highly favourable account of a visit - and a history of the boiled egg.

Baked raspberry cheesecake

Soft fruit from the garden is used in many summer dishes at Hunter's, and raspberries are always a special treat. The coulis is simply liquidised soft fruit, sieved to remove pips and sweetened to taste (about 2oz / 50g caster sugar per 8oz / 225g fruit); sharpen with a little lemon juice if you like. It can be made with any soft fruit, and is a useful accompaniment for ice creams and many other dishes.

Serves 10-12
Filling:
1¹/₂lb / 675g Philadelphia cream
  cheese
7 whole eggs
8oz / 225g caster sugar
18fl oz / ¹/₂litre / 2¹/₄ cups raspberry
  coulis
Base:
1 large packet digestive biscuits
2oz / 50g / ¹/₂ stick unsalted butter
pinch of ground ginger
To serve:
fresh raspberries, whipped cream

Preheat a warm oven, 325°F / 160°C / gas mark 3

To make the filling: Cream the cheese, eggs and sugar together thoroughly, then blend in the coulis to make a smooth mixture.

To make the base: Melt the butter, and crush the biscuits. Add the melted butter and ginger to the biscuit crumbs and and mix together.

Line a 12 inch / 30 cm spring base tin with tinfoil and baking parchment. Tip the biscuit mixture into the tin and pat down well with the back of a metal spoon to make a base layer.

To bake: Pour in the filling, place the tin in a roastiing tin or similar container, add hot water to come half way up the sides of the cheesecake tin (to make a bain marie) and cook in the preheated oven for about 40 - 50 minutes, or until it feels firm to the touch. When cooked, remove the cheesecake from the oven and allow it to cool then leave in the fridge for a few hours, in the tin, to set. When set, remove the tin and lining, place the cheesecake on a large serving plate and cut into wedges.

To serve: Place a portion on each dessert plate; decorate with fresh whipped cream and serve with fresh raspberries, and some extra coulis if you like.

Rillette of rabbit
with Cumberland Sauce

Hunter's is known for its down to earth good cooking and dishes like this - which make a refreshing change from the dressed-up fashionable fare in many of Ireland's restaurants today - are typical. This classic sauce partners the rillette perfectly, and is also a very useful accompaniment for many other dishes, including liver patés, terrines and baked ham.

Serves 4
4 saddles of rabbit, on the bone and
*   trimmed*
1 medium sized onion, roughly
*   chopped*
1 clove of garlic, crushed
2 dried bay leaves
1¹/₂ pints / 900ml / 4 cups water
6 whole black peppercorns;
3 large tbsp / 3³/₄ large US
*   tablespoons mayonnaise*
1 large tbsp / 1¹/₄ large tablespoons
*   French mustard*
4oz / 110g / 1 stick plus 1 US
*   tablespoon melted butter*
bunch of parsley, chopped
Sea salt & freshly ground black
*   pepper.*
For the sauce:
1 pint / 600ml / 2³/₄ cups orange
*   juice*
¹/₂pint / 300ml / 1¹/₃ cups lemon juice
2fl oz / 60 ml / 4 US tablespoons port
1 small jar of redcurrant jelly,
*   preferably home-made*
zest of 2 oranges
zest of 1 lemon
Melba Toast:
4 slices white bread (crusts removed)

Place the rabbit in a casserole with the onion, garlic, bay leaves, water and peppercorns. Bring to the boil and simmer for 20-30 minutes. Remove rabbit and cool. Remove the meat from the bones and place in a blender. Add the mayonnaise, mustard, butter and parsley. Season to taste with sea salt and freshly ground pepper. Blend together to a fairly chunky consistency. Remove from the blender and store in the fridge until required.

To make the sauce: Place the orange juice, lemon juice, port and redcurrant jelly in a saucepan and reduce until the it reaches the consistency of syrup. Add the orange and lemon zest. Allow to cool. Serve in a sauceboat or drizzle over salad.

To make Melba Toast: Toast bread lighty on both sides, split in half through centre and cut into triangles; season, then grill untoasted sides until browned and curling.

To serve: Spoon the rillettes onto four serving plates. Garnish with rocket, radicchio or oak leaf lettuce, and thyme flowers, and serve accompanied by Melba Toast and Cumberland Sauce.

The King Sitric Restaurant

Howth, Co Dublin

Perfectly poised at the end of the East Pier, where chef-patron Aidan MacManus can keep an eye on his lobster pots in Balscadden Bay on one side and the fishing boats coming into harbour on the other, The King Sitric is named after an 11th century Norse King of Dublin, and is one of Dublin's longest established fine dining restaurants. Menus depend on the availability of the fresh seafood landed daily but, in winter, when gales can keep the fishing boats in harbour for days at a time, game is also another treat in the repertoire. Other house specialities include shellfish of all kinds, notably crab and lobster, and the dessert 'Meringue Sitric' which was invented to make use of all the egg whites left over after making yolk-rich sauces for fish - and a brown bread recipe handed down through generations of Aidan's family. Renovations completed a few years ago allowed major changes at the King Sitric, including the relocation of dining areas to the first floor to maximise on the sea views, the addition of a unique temperature controlled wine cellar to house Aidan's treasured bottles (the King Sitric wine list is renowned), and also some very comfortable accommodation.

Lobster Lawyer

This classic lobster dish has an Irish whiskey and cream sauce. The basic cooking method given here can be applied to many other lobster dishes if longer time is allowed for boiling - 12 minutes per lb / 450g for an average lobster (1-1½lb / 450-700g), half this time if it is to be split and grilled.

Serves 1 as a main course, 2 as a starter
1 lobster (about 1½lb / 700g in weight)
a little oil
1 wedge of lemon
1 heaped tsp Dijon mustard
a generous splash of Irish whiskey
2fl oz / 60ml / 4 US tablespoons cream
Freshly ground pepper

Plunge the lobster into boiling water for approximately 90 seconds. This will kill the lobster quickly and loosen the flesh from the shell. Allow to cool then remove the claws, tearing them gently from the body. Remove the rubber bands and break off the knuckles; break them in half and remove the meat with a pick. Next place the claws on a chopping board and with the back of a heavy knife crack down on each claw, rotating it all the way round; 3 or 4 hits should be sufficient. Remove the meat and set aside.

Put the lobster on the board and place the tip of the knife just beneath the cross on the lobster's head; insert and cut along the tail until you have cut right through, then reverse and continue to cut through to the head. Remove the sack and creamy bits at the top of the head, and discard. Remove the meat and set aside.

Rinse the shells for re-use, and keep warm. You will notice that the meat is very rare (raw); cut it into small pieces, place in a sauté pan and warm gently with a little olive oil. Squeeze the lemon juice over the lobster, stir in a heaped teaspoon of Dijon mustard and a generous splash of Irish whiskey, warmed in a tablespoon, and then lighted. Allow the whiskey to flame until it goes out, then add the cream, season with freshly ground pepper only and bring to the boil. Let it simmer just long enough to reduce the sauce to the desired consistency.

To serve: Using a slotted spoon, remove the meat and place into the warmed shells, then pour the sauce on top and serve immediately.

Oysters Bloody Mary

Aidan MacManus uses native west coast oysters for this dish whenever possible, although rock oysters - which are farmed not far away in Carlingford Lough - can be used instead. When using rock oysters, select them as small as possible.

Serves 1 as a light main course, 2 as a starter

12 oysters
6 tomatoes
1 tbsp / 1¼ US tablespoons of vodka
a dash of Tabasco
a double dash of Worcestershire sauce
the juice of half a lemon
1 red chilli pepper, chopped
a little cucumber, skinned and seeded

First make the Bloody Mary: Blanch the tomatoes, then skin them and discard the pulp. Finely dice two of the tomatoes and leave aside. Put the rest in a liquidiser with the vodka, Tabasco and Worcestershire sauce, lemon juice and the red chilli pepper. Liquidise. Take the diced tomatoes and add an equal amount of diced, seeded and skinned cucumber. Add to the juice and refrigerate until required.

To prepare the oysters: Using an oyster knife, carefully open the oysters over a bowl to catch the juices. Loosen and turn the oyster in its shell, then strain any juices and return to their shells. Cover with about a tablespoon of the Blood Mary sauce and chill for about 30 minutes.

To serve: Arrange the oysters by the half dozen, on oyster plates if available. Serve with a wedge of lemon, and offer some freshly baked brown bread on the side.

L'Ecrivain Restaurant

Lower Baggot Street, Dublin 2

Chef-patron Derry Clarke and his wife, Sallyanne, have run their light and airy restaurant in the heart of Georgian Dublin since 1989, and they have since won many accolades for its unique combination of chic contemporary style, Derry's imaginative cooking, and service that is exceptionally well-informed yet also warm and friendly. Derry is renowned for his commitment to the best of Irish seasonal produce and his cooking style - classic French with a strong leaning towards modern Irish cooking - is perhaps best expressed in dishes like a wonderful signature starter of baked rock oysters with York cabbage, crispy cured bacon and a Guinness sabayon. Seafood is a special strength - fish from all around Ireland is cooked here on the same day as it is caught - and many speciality foods from small Irish producers feature in season. Attention to detail shows in everything from the delicious home-baked breads to mature farmhouse cheeses and wonderful puddings are presented with panache.

Glazed peach on a buttermilk & strawberry parfait, with hazelnut biscuits

This lovely dessert makes the most of two luscious summer fruits. The buttermilk gives a delicious 'bite' to the strawberry parfait, and the crisp nutty biscuits partner the fruits perfectly.

Serves 6
5 fl oz / 150ml / ³/4 cup white wine
10 fl oz / 300ml / 1¹/3 cups water
1 vanilla pod
8oz / 225g / 1 cup caster sugar
6 peaches, peeled

Parfait:
4 egg yolks
5oz / 150g / ²/3 cup sugar
2oz / 50g glucose or golden syrup
4 fl oz / 100 ml / ¹/2 cup strawberry coulis
1 tbsp / 1¹/4 US tablespoons water
18 fl oz / 500ml / 2¹/4 cups cream, whipped
7oz / 200g / 1 cup strawberries, roughly chopped
9 fl oz / 250ml / 1 cup plus 2 US tablespoons buttermilk

Hazelnut biscuits:
9oz / 250g / 2 cups flour
9oz / 250g / 2¹/4 sticks unsalted butter, at room temperature
5oz / 150g / 1 cup plus 2 scant US tablespoons icing sugar
2oz / 50g / ¹/2 cup hazelnuts, chopped
1 egg white

First make the parfait: Whisk the egg yolks until thick. Place the sugar, glucose or golden syrup, strawberry coulis (fresh strawberries, puréed and strained) and water in a saucepan. Heat gently until sugar is dissolved, then bring to the boil and cook for 2-5 minutes over a moderate heat, until the bubbling mixture becomes denser. Add this syrupy mixture to the eggs, whisking continuously until thick. Fold in the whipped cream, chopped strawberries and buttermilk. Place in a mould and freeze for 3 hours before using.

Next, make the biscuits: Beat the flour, butter and icing sugar together, then blend in the hazelnuts and egg white. Form this mixture into a ball, wrap in cling film, and refrigerate for 30 minutes.

Meanwhile, preheat a hot oven, 400°F / 200°C / gas mark 6.

Roll out the dough thinly, cut it into discs and lay on a greased baking tray. Bake for 6-8 minutes until golden brown. Remove the tray from the oven and allow the biscuits to cool a little before transferring to a rack to cool.

To prepare the glazed peaches: Heat the wine, water, sugar and vanilla pod gently until the sugar has completely dissolved, then boil, uncovered, until you have a syrupy mixture. Add the peaches and poach for 8-10 minutes, or until just tender. Lift the peaches out and keep warm. To reduce the syrup, boil again until thick and golden.

To serve: De-mould the parfait, returning any surplus to the freezer immediately. Glaze the warm peaches with the syrup, and arrange them on dessert plates with the parfait and the hazelnut biscuits.

Cured wild Irish salmon with whiskey yoghurt and sweet mustard dressings

In this house variation on the Scandinavian gravadlax, the salmon is 'cured' in a mixture of sugar, salt and flavourings. Do not be daunted by the dramatic restaurant presentation, as it is actually very simple to prepare at home, and makes an excellent dinner party starter.

Serves 6-8

For the cured salmon:

2lb / 900g tail end fillet of wild salmon, scaled, with the skin on
3 tbsp / 3³/4 US tablespoons sugar
1¹/2 tbsp / 2 US tablespoons coarse sea salt
1 tbsp / 1¹/4 US tablespoons fresh dill, chopped
a sprinkling of crushed white peppercorns

For the dressings:

5fl oz / 150ml / ¹/2 cup wholegrain mustard
2 tbsp / 2¹/2 US tablespoons honey
4¹/2oz / 125g tub of natural yoghurt
half measure of Irish whiskey

Garnish:

salad leaves of your choice

First, prepare the salmon: Mix the curing ingredients - sugar, salt, chopped dill and crushed peppercorns - and sprinkle over the flesh side of the salmon. Wrap in cling film and refrigerate for 12 hours (farmed salmon takes 24 hours as it has more fat).

To make the dressings: Mix mustard and honey together; mix yoghurt and whisky together.

To assemble the dish: Arrange some salad leaves on serving plates. Slice the salmon thinly and arrange on top. Drizzle some mustard dressing around the edge of the plate, and serve with the whiskey yoghurt.

Lisdonagh House

Caherlistrane, Headford, Co Galway

Beautifully situated in the heart of hunting and fishing country about 20 minutes drive north of Galway city, Lisdonagh House is set in over 100 acres of woodland on an elevated site with views over Lake Hackett. It is a lovely early Georgian property, with a stunning oval entrance hall with late eighteeenth century murals depicting the four virtues, large well-proportioned reception rooms and a fine staircase - and the house has recently been restored to a high level of comfort, with due respect for its period features. Luxurious bedrooms, furnished with antiques and decorated in period style,with marbled bathrooms to match, are named after prominent Irish writers and artists. Fresh seafood is a speciality, and their own kitchen garden supplies fresh vegetables and herbs for residents' dinners served in the elegantly appointed dining room.

Lisdonagh nutty brown bread

Always a great breakfast favourite. They use Howard's wholemeal flour to make this crusty loaf at Lisdonagh; it has quite a coarse texture and works especially well with the walnuts. It is important to work quickly and lightly when making soda breads, putting the bread into the oven as soon as possible after the buttermilk is added to the dry ingredients. Soda breads are best eaten on the day of baking, but cut better if left for a few hours before slicing.

Makes one round loaf
2lb 3oz / 1kg / 8¹/₂ cups wholemeal flour (firmly packed)
2 heaped tsp bicarbonate of soda, sifted
1 heaped tsp baking powder, sifted
a pinch of salt
1 tbsp / 1¹/₄ tablespoons brown sugar
4oz / 110g / 1 cup walnuts, chopped
1¹/₂ pt / 900ml / 4 cups buttermilk

Preheat a fairly hot, 375°F / 190°C / gas mark 5.

Mix all of the dry ingredients together in a large bowl. Add the buttermilk and mix lightly until you have a soft but not too wet dough. Turn on to a floured worktop and shape into a round, then place on a greased and floured baking tray. Cut a cross in the top to ensure even cooking, then bake in the preheated oven for about 45 minutes or until the bread is well risen and nicely browned - when you tap the base of the loaf lightly, it should sound hollow. Cool on a wire rack (wrapped in a clean tea towel if you prefer a soft crust).

Vegetable spring rolls

These spring rolls make a tasty vegetarian starter.

Serves 6-10
1 pack x 30 Thai spring roll pastry
Filling:
1 red pepper, thinly sliced
1 green pepper, thinly sliced
2 large carrot, cut into julienne
1 baby marrow, cut into julienne
1 onion, thinly sliced
2 scallions, quartered
3^1/$_2$ oz / 100g / 2 cups shitaki
*   mushrooms, thinly sliced*
2oz / 50g / 1 cup bean sprouts
1 tbsp / 1^1/$_4$ US tablespoons garlic,
*   crushed*
1 tsp fresh ginger, finely chopped
1 tbsp / 1^1/$_4$ US tablespoons oil;
7 fl oz / 200ml / scant cup soy sauce
1 tbsp / 1^1/$_4$ US tablespoons sesame
*   oil*

Chilli jam dipping sauce:
8oz / 225g / 1 cup sugar
18fl oz / 500ml / 2^1/$_4$ cups water
2-3 large chilli (to taste)
1 tbsp / 1^1/$_4$ US tablespoons fresh
*   ginger, chopped*
^{1}/$_2$ tbsp / ^{3}/$_4$ US tablespoon chopped
*   garlic*
3 tbsp / 3^3/$_4$ US tablespoons tomato
*   sauce*
2oz / 50g / 1 cup fresh coriander,
*   chopped*

First make the sauce: Heat the sugar and water together, stirring to dissolve the sugar, then bring to the boil. Add the remaining ingredients, and boil until reduced by half. Allow to cool, then pour into a suitable container and store in the fridge, where it will keep for two weeks.

For the filling: In a very hot pan, stir-fry all the ingredients, except the soy sauce and sesame oil, for about 5 minutes. Stir in the soy sauce and sesame oil and fry for one more minute. Cool, and strain off any liquid.

To make the spring rolls: Place 2 heaped teaspoons of the vegetable mixture in a sausage shape in the centre of each spring roll pastry. Egg wash the edges, then fold and roll to make each small spring roll.

Deep fry in hot oil, preheated to 150°C / 300°F, until golden.

To serve: Arrange three to five spring rolls per person on serving plates with a salad garnish and lemon wedges. Use the dipping sauce as a garnish, or offer it separately.

Longueville House

Mallow, Co Cork

The history of this fine house is wonderfully romantic, "the history of Ireland in miniature", and it's a story with a happy ending: having lost their lands in the Cromwellian Confiscation, the O'Callaghans took up ownership again some 300 years later. The present house, an elegant Georgian mansion of pleasingly human proportions dating from 1720, (with wings and the lovely Turner conservatory, recently renovated, added later) overlooks the ruins of their original home, Dromineen Castle. The warm, informal hospitality of the O'Callaghans - Michael and Jane, their son William and his wife Aisling - is essential to the spirit of Longueville, which opened its doors to guests in 1967 and was one of the first Irish country houses to do so. The River Blackwater, farm and garden supply William's kitchen with salmon, the famous Longueville lamb and organic fruit and vegetables - and Michael O'Callaghan's great enthusiasm and the estate's crowning glory (well, in years when the weather is kind anyway), their own house wine, a light refreshing white fittingly named "Coisreal Longueville".

Murphy's and walnut bread

Murphy's stout is made in Cork, and adds a special flavour to this house speciality which is an unusual combination of styles - the method is very like traditional Irish soda bread, but fresh yeast is used as the raising agent instead of bread soda and buttermilk.

Makes two loaves

8fl oz / 225ml / 1 cup Murphy's (stout)
8fl oz / 225ml / 1 cup warm water
1 tbsp / 1¼ US tablespoons treacle,
1½ oz / 40g fresh yeast
1¾lb / 800g / 7 cups (firmly packed) wholemeal flour,
1 tsp salt,
2 tbsp / 2½ US tablespoons walnuts, chopped

In a saucepan, warm the stout and water to about blood temperature. (If overheated it will kill the yeast in the stout.) Remove from the heat, whisk in the treacle and then the yeast, making sure it dissolves into the stout completely. Mix the flour, salt and walnuts together. Make a well in the centre, and add the wet ingredients. Mix well to make a fairly soft, pliable dough; adjust with a little extra water or flour if it seems too dry or too wet. Divide the mixture in two, and place in two buttered loaf tins, 8 inch / 20cm x 4 inch / 10cm. Leave in a warm place for about 1 hour, to rise.

Meanwhile, pre-heat a moderate oven, 330°F / 170°C / gas mark 3.

Bake the loaves in the preheated oven for 45 minutes, then remove them from the tins and turn upside-down on oven rack; continue baking for a further 15 minutes, or until the loaves sound hollow when rapped on the base with your knuckles. Cool on a wire rack.

Breast of chicken with a herb & cumin stuffing and thyme sauce

William O'Callaghan uses local free range chicken and herbs straight from the walled garden for this tasty dish - and, despite the long list of ingredients, it is not difficult to make and would be a good recipe for a dinner party.

Serves 8
8 medium sized chicken breasts, skin on (try to ensure that there is extra skin left on at head end of breast)

Stuffing:
1 tbsp / 1¼ US tablespoons olive oil
9oz / 250g / 2 cups onion, finely chopped
2 cloves of garlic, peeled and crushed
11oz / 300g / 3 sticks butter, cubed
5oz / 150g / 3 cups fresh breadcrumbs
½ tsp ground cumin
1 tsp salt
½ tsp freshly ground white pepper
5oz / 150g / 3 cups parsley, freshly chopped
1 tsp thyme, chopped
1 tsp tarragon, chopped

For frying the chicken:
2oz / 50g / ½ stick butter
1 tbsp olive oil

Sauce:
10fl oz / 300ml / 1⅓ cups dry white wine
3⅓ pints / 1.5 litres / 6¾ cups brown chicken stock, boiling hot
1 tsp thyme, chopped

First make the stuffing: Heat the olive oil in a medium sized saucepan, then gently fry the onion and garlic in it without colouring, until soft. Add the butter and melt it, then add the breadcrumbs, cumin and seasoning and mix together well. Finally, add the chopped herbs, and mix well again. Place the mixture in a bowl and allow to cool, then put into the fridge. When cold, divide the stuffing roughly into eight balls with your hands.

To stuff the chicken breasts: Remove any excess fat from under the flap of skin (at the head end) on the chicken breasts. To insert the filling underneath the skin, begin at the flap and use your index finger to create a cavity between the skin and the flesh, taking care not to puncture the skin. Roll the stuffing balls into cylinders. (The length should be about the width of the palm of your hand.) Place the filling into the cavity and use your fingers to mould it back into a ball shape. Enclose the filling by tucking the flap of skin under the flesh side.

Preheat a fairly hot oven, 400°F / 200°C / gas mark 6.

To cook: In an ovenproof frying pan, heat a tablespoon of the olive oil and 50g / ½ stick butter over a fairly high heat. Season the chicken breasts and cook flesh side down until coloured, spooning some of the butter and oil over the skin to colour it. Transfer the pan to the oven and continue cooking for about 15 minutes. (Juices will run clear when pierced, without any pink traces of blood.) When done, rest in a warm place on a rack set over a dish for about 8 minutes. Save any juices for the sauce.

To prepare sauce: While the chicken is resting, drain the fat from the pan and deglaze with the white wine; boil to reduce the volume to 2fl oz / 50ml / ¼ cup. Add the hot chicken stock and boil briskly until reduced to about 14fl oz / 400ml / 1¾ cups, then add the thyme.

To serve: Cut each chicken breast diagonally into two pieces, and present it on heated plates, with one piece resting on the other. Serve with a selection of seasonal vegetables.

Marlfield House

Gorey, Co Wexford

A magnificent retreat, where discerning guests from all corners of the world come to be pampered, this fine Regency period mansion was built around 1830 for the Earl of Courtown and converted by its present owners, the Bowe family, to create this exceptional small hotel. To call Mary Bowe's interiors luxurious fails to do justice to the level of grandeur at Marlfield, especially in the suites - and, naturally, standards of service and food match the surroundings. The restaurant is one of the country's most elegant formal dining rooms, with a lovely airy atmosphere and delightful trompe l'oeil greenery blending effortlessly into a period-style conservatory and thence into immaculately maintained gardens, complete with ornamental lake. Carefully tended kitchen gardens, which supply much of the fresh fruit, vegetables and herbs required by the house, are also a point of interest for guests who can go and see for themselves the good things which will later make such a striking appearance at dinner.

Macaroons with lemon posset

This is a very good way of using up egg whites. At Marlfield, macaroons are served with this lemon posset, or for afternoon tea. They keep for 4-5 days in an airtight container.

Makes about 12
For the macaroons:
4¹/₂oz / 120g / 1 cup ground almonds
4¹/₂oz / 120g / 1 cup icing sugar
2 small egg whites
For the lemon posset:
4oz / 110g sugar
³/₄ pint / 450 ml cream
Juice of 3 lemons

Preheat a moderate oven, 350°F / 180°C / gas mark 4.

To make the macaroons: Mix the ground almonds and sifted icing sugar in a mixing bowl. Add the egg whites and mix until the mixture comes together. Pipe onto a baking tray lined with greaseproof paper (or put the mixture out in tablespoonfuls) and bake in the preheated oven for about 10 minutes, or until golden. Remove with a spatula and cool on a wire rack.

To make the posset: Put the sugar and cream into a saucepan, heat gently to dissolve the sugar then bring to the boil. Add the juice of the lemons (which will react with the cream to set the mixture), then strain and allow to cool. Leave in the fridge to set, and serve with the macaroons.

Smoked Abbey Brie fritters
with rhubarb chutney

Serves 4
For the fritters:
2 x 200g / 7oz wheels of smoked
  Abbey Brie
a little plain white flour
2 eggs, beaten
about 4 oz / 110g / 2 cups white
  breadcrumbs
For the rhubarb chutney:
1lb / 450g rhubarb, trimmed and
  sliced
12oz / 350g / 3 cups onions, peeled
  and sliced
6oz / 175g / 1 cup plus 2 US
  tablespoons raisins
13oz / 375g / 1³/4 cups brown sugar
³/4 pint / 450ml / 2 cups cider vinegar
3 tsp salt
1 tsp ground cinnamon
1 tsp ground ginger
¹/2 tsp ground cloves
a pinch of cayenne pepper

To make the chutney: Put all the listed ingredients into a stainless steel preserving pan and set over a low heat. Stir with a wooden spoon until the sugar has completely dissolved, then bring to the boil. Stirring frequently, simmer over gentle heat for two hours, or until the chutney has reduced and thickened. Spoon the chutney into warmed sterilised jars. Best kept in a cool dark place for 1 month before using.

To prepare the fritters: Cut the Abbey Brie into 16 wedges. Dust with the flour, then dip first into the beaten egg, and then into the bread crumbs. Heat some fresh oil to 170°C / 325°F and deep fry the fritters for 30 seconds. Drain and serve hot, with a small salad and the chutney.

Moy House

Lahinch, Co Clare

This stunning mid 18th century house just outside Lahinch is on a wooded 15 acre site on the river Moy and enjoys a commanding position overlooking Lahinch Bay, with clear coastal views. Under the present caring ownership, it has undergone major restoration work, completed with admirable sensitivity to the house and its position. It is now one of Ireland's most appealing and luxurious country houses - greatly enhanced by manager Bernie Merry's genuine hospitality and attention to detail. Furnished with wonderful fabrics and antiques, Moy House offers every imaginable comfort and elegant, spacious bedrooms overlooking the Atlantic provide a marvellous retreat for discerning guests. A large, elegant drawing room has an open fire and honesty bar where guests enjoy aperitifs before going downstairs to dinner - a high point of any visit, served in a beautifully appointed dining room with a special quality that makes it a cosy retreat in wild weather. This lovely house offers a unique experience and is worth a special trip.

Pan-fried turbot, Galway Bay prawn, fennel and asparagus, with a citrus sauce

This recipe is very much a restaurant dish but, while it may seem complicated, it is not difficult if taken stage by stage - and any of the stages can easily be simplified for cooking at home.

Serves 4

1¹/₂ lb / 700g turbot fillet (8 x 3oz /
   75g portions, approx.)
20 Galway Bay prawns (langoustines)
1 bulb of fennel
a little olive oil
8 asparagus spears
Salt & freshly milled pepper

Sauce:
Scant 4fl oz / 100ml / ¹/₂ cup fish
   stock
juice of 2 oranges
juice of 1/2 lemon
3¹/₂oz / 100g butter 1 stick butter
¹/₄ pint / 150ml / ²/₃ cup cream

Garnish:
4 tbsp / 5 US tablespoons balsamic
   vinegar
1 courgette
2 small tomatoes, concassé
4 sprigs of fennel

To prepare the fish and vegetables: Wash the turbot; cut into 8 pieces, if necessary; place in the refrigerator until ready to cook. Boil the prawns for 3 minutes, turn into a colander to drain, and remove from their shells. Wash the fennel bulb and slice into rounds; wash the asparagus and trim off the coarse base of the stems.

To make the sauce: Put the fish stock, orange and lemon juice in a saucepan and boil, uncovered, until reduced by one quarter. Add the cream, remove from the heat and gradually incorporate the butter to make a smooth sauce. Set aside.

To prepare the garnish: Simmer the balsamic vinegar in a saucepan until reduced by at least a quarter, and set aside. Wash the courgette and use a small knife to turn it into barrel shapes. Scald and peel the tomatoes, remove core and dice the flesh to make tomato concassé.

To cook: Fry the fennel in a little olive oil for 3 minutes; boil the asparagus for 3 minutes; boil the courgettes in salted water for 2 minutes. Brush the turbot lightly with olive oil; heat a dry pan and, when very hot, place the turbot skin side down and sear for 2 minutes. Turn over and sear the other side then lower the heat and cook for about a further 2 minutes. Add the prawns for a few moments to reheat.

To serve: Place the fennel in the centre of four heated plates, then place two spears of asparagus on top, then a piece of turbot, five prawns and finally the second portion of turbot. Place the turned courgettes and tomato concassé around the fish and spoon the citrus sauce around the plate. Flash under the grill, and finish with sprig of fennel and a drizzle of balsamic reduction.

Pesto, sun-dried tomato and caramelised onion foccacia

This herby bake is a popular bread at Moy House.

Makes 1 loaf

11oz / 300g / 2¹/₂ cups plain white flour

¹/₂ tsp salt

7g / 2 tsp easy bake (fast action) yeast

1oz / 25g / 2 scant US tablespoons Parmesan cheese, grated

1 tbsp / 1¹/₄ US tablespoons fresh sage, chopped

1 tbsp / 1¹/₄ US tablespoons fresh rosemary, chopped

2 tsp fresh parsley, chopped

2 tbsp / 2¹/₂ US tablespoons olive oil

9 fl oz / 250ml / 1 cup plus 2 US tablespoons tepid water

5oz / 150g chopped onion

1 tbsp / 1¹/₄ US tablespoons basil pesto

2oz / 50g sun-dried tomatoes

Sift the flour and salt into a large bowl, stir in the yeast, cheese and herbs. Pour in the oil and water, gradually stir in the flour, mix to a soft dough. Turn onto a floured surface and knead for about 4 minutes or until the dough feels silky to the touch. Place on a greased baking tray, press to shape into a 10in / 25cm circle and cover with oiled cling film. Leave to prove at room temperature for 1 hour, or until the dough doubles in size.

Meanwhile, preheat a hot oven, 400°F / 200°C / gas mark 6.

Cook the onions gently in a little oil, until caramelised.

When the dough is ready to bake, very gently spread the pesto onto the top, then add the onions and tomatoes and bake in the hot oven for 25 minutes. Cool on wire rack, and serve in slices.

Moyglare Manor

Maynooth, Co Kildare

Just eighteen miles from Dublin, neatly manicured hedging and rolling parkland give way to half a mile of tree-lined avenue leading to this imposing Georgian manor with commanding views over the surrounding countryside. Once inside it quickly becomes obvious that the owner, Norah Devlin, lavishes her love of beautiful things on the place - her passsion for antiques has become legendary. Gilt-framed mirrors and portaits are everywhere shown to advantaqe aqainst deep-shaded damask walls and the remarkable abundance of chairs and sofas of every pedigree ensures there is always comfortable seating, no matter how busy the restaurant. It's a little like being in an immaculately maintained antique shop. Excellent food and service is complemented by an exceptional wine list, ensuring a memorable wining and dining experiences tor the connoisseur. Accommodation is equally special, in luxurious - and, yes, antique-filled - rooms.

Poached duo of fresh cod and salmon with a fresh prawn, white wine & herb cream

This dish is a great favourite at Moyglare, and is very easy to make if you get your local fishmonger to fillet and debone the fish, and shell the prawns for you. Dublin Bay prawns (langoustines) are suggested, but you could use other large prawns, as available.

Serves 4
1$^3/4$ pints / 1 litre / 4$^1/2$ cups fish stock or bouillon, for poaching
4 x 4oz / 110g chunky cod pieces, skinned and pin-boned
4 x 4oz / 110g salmon fillet, skinned and pin-boned

Sauce:
a little butter
12oz / 340g fresh Dublin Bay prawns, shelled
1 glass of dry white wine
1 pint / 600ml / 2$^3/4$ cups cream
4 tbsp / 5 US tablespoons chives, chopped
4 tbsp / 5 US tablespoons parsley, chopped
4 bay leaves
1 tbsp / 1$^1/4$ US tablespoons arrowroot or cornflour (optional)
salt and freshly ground pepper

Garnish:
chopped flat parsley and chives

First make the sauce: Put a little butter into a hot pan and briefly sauté the prawns in it; remove the prawns when just half-cooked, and set aside. Add the wine and simmer to reduce the volume by one third. Add the cream and herbs, season with salt and pepper and simmer for 8 to 10 minutes. If you feel the sauce is still too thin, it may be thickened with about a tablespoon of arrowroot (or cornflour), slaked in a little water before adding in to the hot liquid. Keep warm and, just before serving, return the reserved prawns to the sauce for about 2 minutes, to finish cooking.

To cook the fish: Bring the poaching liquid to the boil, then add the salmon and cod; bring back to boiling point and then simmer for about 5 minutes, or until just cooked.

To serve: Arrange the salmon and cod on heated plates, pour the sauce (with the prawns) over the fish and garnish with parsley and chives.

Tiramisu

Moyglare Manor has a reputation for delicious desserts - and this more-ish and easy-to-make Italian style trifle is deservedly popular.

Serves 6
5 eggs, separated
4^1/$_2$oz / 125g / ^{1}/$_2$ cup caster sugar
9oz / 250g / 1 cup mascarpone
  cheese
18fl oz / 500 ml / 2^1/$_4$ cups strong
  black coffee
3fl oz / 100ml / scant ^{1}/$_2$ cup Marsala
9oz / 250g boudoir biscuits (sponge
  fingers)
cocoa powder, for dusting

Using an electric mixer, whisk the egg yolks well with the caster sugar, until light and creamy, then blend in the mascarpone. In a separate bowl, whisk the egg whites, until stiff, then use a large metal spoon to fold them carefully into the yolk mixture. Mix the coffee and Marsala and, using a shallow dish, briefly soak the sponge biscuit in this mixture. Select a large glass dish, or generous individual stemmed glasses, and layer the boudoir biscuits with the two mixtures, finishing with a layer of the marscapone mixture.

Just before serving, sprinkle lightly with cocoa powder.

The Mustard Seed at Echo Lodge

Ballingarry, Co Limerick

The picture postcard village of Adare was the first home to Dan Mullane's pretty and characterful restaurant The Mustard Seed, which he then moved to these new premises in a spacious Victorian residence just ten minutes drive away, to celebrate its first decade in business, in 1985. Set on ten acres, Echo Lodge has mature trees, shrubberies and an orchard which have since been rejuvenated, and also a kitchen garden which provides abundant quantities of organically grown vegetables, herbs and fruit for the highly acclaimed restaurant. While the main emphasis remains on food, this lovely house also offers luxurious accommodation, allowing Dan to provide the special hospitality that comes so naturally to him. Elegance, comfort and generosity are the key features - seen through decor and furnishings which bear the mark of a seasoned traveller whose eye has found much to delight in while wandering the world.

Gratinated warm oysters on a tomato & sweet pepper salsa with St. Tola goat cheese butter

The sweetness of the oysters with the pepper and tomato salsa combine with an outstanding Irish goat cheese to make a superb starter. This salsa is also a good alternative to a cream sauce with any fish, meat, or poultry dish, as is the goat cheese butter, used in the same way or simply on toast.

Serves 4
Goat cheese butter:
2oz / 50g St Tola goat cheese
2oz / 50g /¹/₂ stick butter
Salsa:
1 tomato, skinned, deseeded and diced
¹/₂ red pepper, skinned, deseeded and diced
2 scallions (spring onions), finely chopped
1 small clove garlic, crushed
¹/₂ red onion, finely chopped
¹/₂ tbsp / ³/₄ US tablespoon balsamic vinegar
2 tbsp / 2¹/₂ US tablespoons olive oil seasoning to taste
16 fresh oysters
Garnish:
4 small handfuls of seaweed

To make the goat cheese butter: Combine cheese and butter in a food processor until the mixture turns white. Roll in cling film to form an elongated sausage shape about the diameter of a two euro coin. Refrigerate.

To make the salsa: Combine all the listed ingredients and season to taste.

For the garnish: Shortly before serving, blanch the seaweed. The reaction of the seaweed in boiling water will turn it green.

To assemble the dish: Working over a bowl to catch the juices, open the oysters with an oyster knife, then loosen them from their shell base and remove. Strain any juices collected and return to the shells. Place a teaspoon of salsa in each oyster shell, then replace the oysters and finally top with a coin-sized slice of goat cheese butter. Place under a hot grill and cook until the cheese butter is golden brown.

To serve: Place the freshly blanched seaweed on four warmed plates, then set four grilled oysters each on top of the seaweed.

Porter cake

Served on arrival to guests staying at The Mustard Seed, or as an afternoon indulgence.

Makes one 8 inch / 20cm cake

1 lb / 450g / 4 cups (firmly packed) white flour
1 pinch of salt
1 tsp baking powder
8oz / 225g / 1 cup plus 2 US tablespoons of soft brown sugar
$^1/_2$ tsp nutmeg, freshly grated
$^1/_2$ tsp mixed spice
8oz / 225g / 2$^1/_4$ sticks butter, diced
8oz / 225g / 1$^1/_2$ cups sultanas
8oz / 225g / 1$^1/_2$ cups currants
2oz / 50g / $^1/_2$ cup chopped candied peel
2oz / 50g / $^1/_2$ cup crystallised cherries
$^1/_2$ pint / 300ml / 1$^1/_3$ cups Guinness (stout)
2 medium eggs, lightly beaten

Preheat a moderate oven, 350°F / 180°C / gas mark 4.

Line the base and sides of a deep 8-inch / 20 cm cake tin with baking parchment.

Sieve the flour, salt and baking powder into a bowl. Add the sugar, nutmeg and spices. Rub in the butter (by hand, or with a mixer). Add the fruit. Combine the stout and beaten egg, then pour into the cake mixture and mix well. Turn into the lined tin and bake in the preheated oven for about 2$^1/_2$ hours, or until the cake is nicely browned and feels springy to the touch.

Cool in the tin, then remove the baking parchment and store in an airtight container to use as required.

Newport House

Newport, Co Mayo

For two hundred years this fine property adjoining the town was the home of the O'Donnells, once the Earls of Tir Connell, and it is now acclaimed as an angling centre - you don't have to be a fisherperson to love this distinctively creeper-clad Georgian House overlooking the river and quay, but it must help. It's been close to the hearts of fishing people, including the present owners, Kieran and Thelma Thompson, for many years and fresh fish is a speciality in the restaurant, including a wide variety of sea fish from nearby Achill Island. A fundamental respect for food, its quality and freshness prevails, and the head chef, John Gavin, has created a distinctive cuisine based on fresh produce from their own fishery, garden and farm. Home smoked salmon is a speciality, and fruit, vegetables and herbs come from a walled kitchen garden that has been worked since 1720 and was established before the house was built, so that fresh produce would be on stream for the owners when they moved in. And, predating the current fashion by several centuries, pure spring water has always been piped into the house for drinking and ice-making.

Wild salmon with sorrel sauce

This lovely dish brings together a classic combination of ingredients that are in season together in the Irish countryside and rivers.

Serves 4
4 salmon fillets
salt and freshly ground pepper
juice of 1 lime
a little butter, melted
Sorrel Sauce:
$^1/_2$oz / 10g / 1 US tablespoon butter
2oz / 50g / $^1/_2$ cup shallots, chopped
1 pint / 600ml / 4$^1/_2$ cups fish stock
4fl oz / 120ml / $^1/_2$ cup vermouth
4fl oz / 120ml / $^1/_2$ cup white wine
5fl oz / 150ml / $^2/_3$ cup cream
juice of 1 lemon
2oz / 50g / 1 cup sorrel, shredded
Garnish:
4 tomato roses (optional)

First make the sauce: Melt the butter in a pan. Add the chopped shallots and cook gently to soften a little, then add the stock, vermouth and white wine. Bring to the boil and simmer, uncovered, to reduce the volume by two-thirds. Add the cream, lemon juice and seasoning. Cook again, uncovered, until reduced to coating consistency. Strain, then stir in the shredded sorrel.

For the fish: Season the salmon fillets with salt, pepper and lime juice. Lightly butter a non-stick frying pan, heat and then put in salmon and fry for half a minute on each side to seal without colouring. Brush with melted butter and place under a hot grill for half a minute only - the salmon should be barely cooked through.

To serve: Lay the salmon fillets on hot plates with the sorrel sauce. Garnish with a tomato rose, if you like, and serve with new potatoes and a selection of seasonal vegetables.

Bread & butter pudding
with whiskey sauce

This great variation on a favourite pudding enjoys perennial popularity at Newport House.

Serves 4

12 slices white bread, toasted
2oz / 50g / $\frac{1}{2}$ stick butter
2oz / 50g / $\frac{1}{3}$ cup sultanas, washed
2 eggs
3oz / 75g / $\frac{1}{3}$ cup caster sugar
$\frac{1}{2}$ pint / 300ml / $1\frac{1}{3}$ cups milk
$\frac{1}{2}$ pint / 300ml / $1\frac{1}{3}$ cups cream
1 tsp vanilla essence

Whiskey sauce:

5oz / 150g / $1\frac{1}{2}$ sticks butter
4oz / 110g / $\frac{1}{2}$ cup caster sugar
1 egg
2fl oz / 60ml / 4 US tablespoons
  whiskey

Preheat a cool oven, 300°F / 150°C / gas mark 2.

Lightly grease four ramekins with butter. Using a 2 inch / 5cm cutter, cut the toast into rounds. Butter, then layer into the buttered ramekins, alternating with the sultanas. Whisk the eggs and sugar together, blend in the milk, cream and vanilla essence, then strain into the ramekins. Stand in a roasting tin half-full of hot water and cook in the preheated oven for 45-60 minutes, or until risen and nicely browned.

To make the whiskey sauce: Melt the butter in a saucepan, add the caster sugar and dissolve over gentle heat. Remove from the heat and add the egg, whisking vigorously, then add the whiskey.

To serve: Turn the puddings out onto four heated plates and pour the whiskey sauce over the top. Decorate with fresh fruit in season if you wish.

Park Hotel Kenmare

Kenmare, Co Kerry

Set in the heart of Ireland's most scenic area, this luxurious hotel adjoins Kenmare town and, with views over sloping gardens to the ever-changing mountains across the bay, is ideally located for both convenience and tranquillity - and is now also home to the deluxe destination spa, SÁMAS, which blends healing traditions from east and west with the life enhancing scenery of Kerry, to revive body, mind and soul. Once inside the granite Victorian building, all guests will find a warm welcome (probably from proprietor Francis Brennan, or his brother John, who is General Manager) and the ever-burning fire in the hall will start the process of weaving The Park's special magic: any suggestion of formality in the architecture or antique furnishings is offset by amusing quirks of

taste - despite the constant quest for perfection, for which 'The Park' is renowned, it is surprisingly relaxed. Good food is to the fore of course, and, while there is a new emphasis on simple, healthy food in the spa, a stylishly restrained classicism has characterised this distinguished kitchen under several famous head chefs. Service in the elegant dining room is unfailingly outstanding, yet never pompous, and the views from window tables are simply lovely - a fitting setting for memorable meals.

Luscious fruit salad

Select your own combination of fruits for this simple jewel-like dessert, which is full of natural energy. Stoned cherries, blueberries, black or red currants, loganberries, blackberries, strawberries and raspberries are all suitable.

Serves 6

2lb 3oz / 1 kg mixed soft fruits
1 small orange, washed
$^1/_2$ cinnamon stick
8fl oz / 225ml apple juice
a little clear honey (optional)
a little Cointreau, or other fruit based
   liqueur (optional)

Prepare the fruit according to type: hull and carefully wash berries, and remove cherry stones. Finely pare the orange; squeeze and strain the juice, then put it into a small pan with the rind, cinnamon, apple juice, and honey (if using). Bring gently to the boil and simmer for 3 or 4 minutes to infuse the orange rind and cinnamon. If using cherries, blueberries, currants or loganberries, add them to the hot juices and leave in this liquid to soften as it cools. When cold, remove the orange rind and cinnamon stick. Put the fruits and their juices into a serving bowl or individual glasses, along with the softer fruits, and mix gently, adding a little liqueur if you like. Serve immediately or chill, as preferred; garnish with mint leaves or other decoration of your choice.

Quenelle of Castletownbere crabmeat with watermelon and asparagus salad

This pretty dish is healthy and simple to make - and depends on top quality ingredients for its success.

Serves 4

10oz / 275g / 1¼ cups picked crabmeat (good quality, free from shell)
juice of half a lime
1 tbsp / 1¼ US tablespoons crème fraîche
Tabasco, to taste
fresh herbs (chives, dill, parsley and coriander), chopped
salt and freshly ground pepper

Garnishes:

4 x 3oz / 75g slices watermelon, trimmed weight
6fl oz / 175ml / ⅔ cup balsamic vinegar
24 asparagus tips, blanched
4 sprigs chervil
frisée lettuce (the centre of the head), picked and washed

To make the quenelles: Place the crabmeat, lime juice, crème fraîche, Tabasco and herbs in a bowl; mix and season to taste, checking that no shell remains. Chill until ready to assemble the dish.

To prepare the garnishes: Trim the watermelon and cut into rectangles 2 inch x 3 inch / 5cm x 8cm (approx.). Put the balsamic vinegar into a saucepan and simmer, uncovered, to reduce by half and make a light syrup. Allow to cool.

To serve: Drizzle the balsamic reduction around four serving plates and put the rectangles of watermelon in the centre. Using a dessertspoon to shape them, form four quenelles and place one on top of each slice of watermelon. Arrange the asparagus tips, frisée and sprigs of chervil around the crab, and serve.

Rathmullan House

Rathmullan, Co Donegal

Donegal has an other-worldliness that is increasingly hard to capture in the traditional family holiday areas and, although it has grown considerably recently, the laid-back charm of Rathmullan House - albeit given invisible backbone by the professionalism of the Wheeler family, who have run Rathmullan House since 1961 - somehow symbolises that special sense of place. The gracious early nineteenth century house and its lovely garden setting on the shores of Lough Swilly seem to have something to offer everyone - just as the luxury of the garden suites and new rooms is balanced by the unpretentious old-fashioned comforts of the family rooms at the top of the house, so all kinds of different visitors have a special warmth for Rathmullan which brings them back time and again. Good food plays a central role in the life of this house, which has a traditional walled garden supplying fresh organic produce for the kitchen and a declared commitment to supporting the fine local ingredients which are used creatively in imaginative meals served in the unusual tented Weeping Elm Restaurant, and the informal Cellar Bar.

Seared king scallops
with black pudding and sauce vierge

This is a lovely summer dish based on the best available ingredients: local dive caught scallops in the shell, caught by Lough Swilly fishermen only when in season, and Roscommon black pudding. It can be served as a starter or, by increasing the number of scallops, as a main course.

Serves 4 as a starter
8 fresh large scallops
16 slices Roscommon (or other good quality) black pudding
salt and white pepper
4 tsp olive oil
Sauce Vierge:
3 fl oz / 75ml / ⅓ cup olive oil
1 tsp lemon juice
1 tsp coriander seeds, crushed
8 basil leaves, cut into strips
2 tomatoes, skinned deseeded and diced
Garnish:
a few freshly picked garden herbs - tarragon, chives, chervil

First make the sauce: Heat the oil and lemon juice over a gentle heat. Remove from the heat and add the coriander seeds and basil, and leave to infuse in the warm oil (the tomato is added just before serving).

To prepare the scallops and black pudding: Quickly wash the scallops in cold water, dry well, and refrigerate for at least 30 minutes. When they are firm, remove from the fridge and slice each of them in half; season with a little salt. In a frying pan, heat the olive oil and sauté slices of black pudding until hot through. Heat a little oil in a separate pan and sauté the scallops briefly in it, turning when golden brown; cook them for a total of only about 2 minutes.

To serve: Stir the diced tomatoes into the prepared sauce, and pour about 2 tablespoons onto each plate. Arrange the slices of scallops and black pudding so that they alternate on top; garnish with the herbs, and serve immediately.

Carrageen moss
with a compôte of garden berries

This is a traditional Irish way of using Carrageen moss, a seaweed which is indigenous to the west coast of Ireland, especially the Fanad Peninsula in Co Donegal. This lovely, simple dish is equally at home among the desserts at dinner, or on the renowned Rathmullan breakfast buffet.

Serves 6-8
¹/₄oz / 5g dried carrageen moss
1 tbsp / 1¹/₄ US tablespoons sugar
1 small egg
1¹/₂ pints / 0.9 litres / ³/₄ quart milk
Compôte:
¹/₄pint / 150ml / ³/₄ cup cold water
2 tbsp / 2¹/₂ US tablespoons caster
  sugar
1-1¹/₂lb / 450-700g mixed berries
  (such as strawberries, raspberries,
  blackberries, black currants,
  blueberries, and loganberries)
a little honey (if required)

To make the carrageen pudding: Soften the carrageen in cold water; this also helps to wash it. Strain. Mix the sugar and egg together and set aside. In a saucepan, bring the milk to boiling point then, after shaking off all the excess water, add the carrageen. Stir gently, then turn down the heat to a simmer, and cook, stirring occasionally, for 15 minutes. Whisk in the egg and sugar mixture. Remove from the stove and strain into a clean bowl. Pour into a serving bowl (or into individual dishes); when cool, place in the fridge to set for at least 30-45 minutes.

To prepare the compôte: Put the sugar and water into a saucepan; heat, stirring, to dissolve the sugar, and bring to the boil. Add the berries that need longest cooking (blackcurrants, blueberries, loganberries) and cook gently for about 10 minutes, adding the softer berries towards the end. Taste, and adjust sweetness with a little honey if required. Pour into a serving dish and allow to cool.

To serve: Select a large serving dish and arrange the compôte and carrageen moss on it, to complement each other.

Rathsallagh House

Dunlavin, Co Wicklow

This large, rambling country house is just an hour from south Dublin, but it could be in a different world. It is very professionally operated, yet the O'Flynn family insist that their home is not an hotel and - although there is an 18-hole golf course with clubhouse in the grounds - the gentle rhythms of life around the country house and gardens ensure that the atmosphere is kept decidedly low-key. Day rooms are elegantly furnished in classic country house style, with lots of comfortable seating areas and open fires, and memorable meals based on the best local and home-grown ingredients are served in a dining room that somehow retains a house party atmosphere. Accommodation varies, as is the way with old houses - some rooms are luxurious, others have a special cottagey charm. But, wherever you lay your head, allow time next morning for the magnificent Edwardian breakfast buffet which offers every conceivable good thing, including silver chafing dishes full of reminders of yesteryear - a sight to gladden the heart of guests planning a round of golf, or even a gentle ramble around the beautiful walled gardens.

Rathsallagh's upside down summer berry tart

The gardens at Rathsallagh provide fresh produce for the kitchen all year round and the walled garden is especially productive in summer, when soft fruits are in season. This is one of many ways in which the luscious berries are used.

Serves 6-8
For the caramel:
1lb 5oz / 600g / 2²/₃ cups sugar
8fl oz / 250 ml / 1 cup water
For the filling:
1 lb / 500g mixed summer berries
*   (raspberries, strawberries,*
*   blueberries and blackberries)*
7 egg whites
11oz / 300g / 1¹/₃ cups caster sugar
9oz / 250g / 2 cups plus 1¹/₂ US
*   tablespoons white flour*
9oz / 250g / 2¹/₂ sticks butter, melted

Preheat a moderate oven, 350°F / 180°C / gas mark 4.

First make the caramel: Place the sugar and water in a saucepan, allow the sugar to dissolve, then cook gently until the colour of honey (325°F / 170°C on a sugar thermometer). Pour into a deep round ovenproof flan dish 10-12 inch / 25-30 cm in diameter and leave to cool.

When the caramel has set, lay the berries on top. Whisk the egg whites and sugar together until white and frothy, then add the flour and melted butter, together, to the egg white mixture and whisk in gently.

Pour this mixture over the berries and bake in the preheated oven for 20-25 minutes, or until the top is brown and the berry juice is bubbling out at the edges. Allow to set for about 15-20 minutes before turning out. Serve with whipped cream.

Braised shank of Wicklow lamb with crushed rosemary potatoes, tomatoes and olives

The locally reared Wicklow lamb served at Rathsallagh, is supplied by Doyle's butchers in Dunlavin - and this simple dish, with its sunny Mediterranean influences, is especially popular with guests.

Serves 4

4 lamb shanks, medium-sized
salt and freshly ground pepper
2 tbsp / 2$\frac{1}{2}$ US tablespoons olive oil
1 onion, roughly chopped
1 carrot, roughly chopped
1 leek, roughly chopped
1 bay leaf
$\frac{1}{2}$ bottle of red wine
18fl oz / 500ml / 2$\frac{1}{4}$ cups beef or
  chicken stock
1 tbsp / 1$\frac{1}{4}$ US tablespoons butter
4 x 8fl oz / 225ml cups baby
  potatoes, boiled
1 onion, finely chopped
1 scallion (spring onion), finely
  chopped
1 tsp rosemary, finely chopped
16 sundried tomatoes
16 kalamata olives

Preheat a moderate oven, 325°F / 170°C / gas mark 3.

To cook the lamb: Season the lamb shanks with salt and freshly ground pepper. Heat a flameproof casserole, add a tablespoon of the olive oil and sear the shanks in it until golden brown on all sides. Remove the meat from the pan and set aside. In the same pan, sauté the onion, carrot and leek, with the bay leaf, until wilted. Stir in the wine and stock. Return the shanks to the casserole, cover and cook in the preheated oven for 1 hour, then turn them over carefully and cook for a further 30 minutes, or until the meat is tender and falling off the bone. Place the shanks on a baking tray.

To make the sauce: Strain the cooking liquid into a saucepan and simmer, uncovered, until reduced by about half. Check the flavour as you do this as it may become too salty if reduced too much.

Potatoes: Melt the butter with the remaining olive oil in large frying pan. Sauté the potatoes, onion, scallion and rosemary over a medium heat until the potatoes are heated through and crispy. Add the tomatoes and olives, and heat through. Season to taste with salt and freshly ground pepper.

To assemble the dish: Re-heat the lamb shanks in the the preheated oven (325°F / 170°C / gas mark 3) for about 15 minutes, or until hot and sizzling. Reheat the sauce. Divide the hot potatoes between four heated plates, place the shanks against them, pour the sauce over shank and serve at once.

Restaurant Patrick Guilbaud

Upper Merrion Street, Dublin 2

For almost a quarter of a century this spacious, elegant restaurant in a Georgian townhouse adjoining the Merrion Hotel has been the leading French restaurant in Ireland. It is a lovely dining room, enhanced by a fine collection of Irish art, and opens onto a terrace and landscaped gardens which make a delightful setting for al fresco dining. Head chef Guillaume Lebrun has presided over this fine kitchen since the restaurant opened, and is renowned for modern classic cuisine, based on the best Irish produce in season; his wide-ranging menus include a wonderfully creative 9-course 'Sea & Land' Tasting Menu that celebrates traditional Irish themes with Gallic flair and, at the other end of the spectrum, a daily table d'hôte lunch menu offers the best value fine dining in Dublin. Service, under the relaxed supervision of Restaurant Manager Stéphane Robin, is invariably immaculate and Patrick Guilbaud himself is usually present to greet guests personally. Every capital city has its great restaurant and this is Dublin's: Restaurant Patrick Guilbaud sets the standard by which all others are judged.

Sea bream 'à la plancha' with fennel & lemon confit

Ask your fishmonger to scale and fillet the sea bream - you could use John Dory instead if it is more easily available.

Serves 4

2 x 1¹/₄lb / 600g sea bream, scaled & filleted (4 fillets)
2oz / 50g / ¹/₂ cup shallots, diced
olive oil
1 clove garlic, crushed
1 bay leaf
1 sprig of thyme
4 fl oz / 100ml / ¹/₂ cup white wine
7 fl oz / 200m / 1 scant cup of chicken stock
8 heads of baby fennel, trimmed
4 spring onions (scallions), trimmed
2 slices of orange peel
3¹/₂oz / 100g / 1 stick cold butter
3¹/₂oz / 100g lemon confit (or 2 oz / 50g lemon segments, skinned)
4 sundried tomatoes
1 tbsp / ³/₄ US tablespoon olive oil
4 slices of dried lemon to garnish (optional)

Sweat the shallots in a little olive oil, add the crushed garlic, bay leaf and thyme, and cook for 1 minute or until the shallots are translucent. Add the wine and reduce by half. Add the stock, bring to the boil, then add the fennel, with the spring onions, and cook until tender. Remove the fennel and spring onions, and keep warm. Add the orange peel and cook uncovered, to reduce the liquid by half. Remove the bay leaf, thyme and orange peel, then add the cold butter and whisk for 1 minute.

To cook the sea bream: Heat a pan over fairly high heat, add a little olive oil and pan fry the fish, skin side down, for 2 minutes; turn over and cook for a further 30 seconds.

To serve: Place the fennel in four large heated soup plates. Add the lemon segments to the sauce and pour it over the fennel. Place the sea bream on top, decorate with some sun-dried tomatoes and a ring of dried lemon, and serve immediately

Tarte sablée au chocolat

Desserts are a speciality at Restaurant Patrick Guilbaud, and this moreish chocolate tart is typical of the treats in store.

Serves 6
Pastry:
3¹/₂oz / 100g / 1 stick butter, at room temperature
3oz / 75g / ¹/₃ cup sugar
1 egg
5oz / 150g / 1¹/₄ cups flour
Chocolate filling:
5oz / 150g dark chocolate
1 egg and 2 egg yolks
1oz / 25g / 2 US tablespoons caster sugar
3¹/₂oz / 100g / 1 stick unsalted butter, softened
a little icing sugar

First, make the pastry case: Mix the butter, sugar and egg together in a bowl for 1 minute. Add the flour and knead the mixture for 1 minute to incorporate thoroughly. Shape into a ball, wrap in cling film, and leave it to rest for 2 hours in the fridge.

Preheat a moderate oven, 350°F / 180°C / gas mark 4.

When ready to bake: Roll out the pastry very thinly and line an 8 inch / 20cm baking tin with it. Place greaseproof paper inside and add some dry lentils, then bake blind in the preheated oven for 10 minutes.

To make the filling: Melt the chocolate slowly in a bowl over hot (not boiling) water. In a mixing bowl, whisk the egg, egg yolks and sugar at high speed for 3 minutes. Then reduce the speed to slow, add the melted chocolate and the softened butter and mix well.

To finish the tart: Remove the greaseproof paper and lentils from the pastry case, and fill with the chocolate mixture. Cook in the preheated oven (350°F / 180°C / gas mark 4) for 8 to 10 minutes, until set. Remove from the oven and allow to cool slightly.

To serve: Dust with icing sugar and serve lukewarm, cut into wedges and accompanied with some vanilla ice cream.

Rosleague Manor

Letterfrack, Co Galway

Set in 30 acres of secluded landscaped gardens planted with rare shrubs and plants, this graciously proportioned Regency house overlooks a tidal inlet towards Ballinakill Bay and conveys a deep sense of peace. Although the area offers plenty of activity for the energetic - salmon, trout and sea fishing, golf and horseriding are all available nearby - the tranquillity of the place makes it hard to imagine anywhere better simply to recharge the soul. Or, for that matter, the body, as fresh seafood and home-grown vegetables and fruit are a speciality - and, of course the famous Connemara lamb. Fine furniture and paintings, peat fires, good food and seclusion from the world add up to make Rosleague a very special place.

Wild Connemara salmon tartare

Simple is as simple does in a magnificently understated starter that owes its success to the exceptional quality of the local ingredients sourced.

Serves 4
9oz / 250g wild salmon fillet
juice of 1 lemon
1 tbsp / ¼ US tablespoon fresh
  coriander, chopped
1 tbsp / 1¼ US tablespoons fresh
  parsley, chopped
1 tbsp / 1¼ US tablespoons olive oil
a dash of Tabasco
a little salt
a little cayenne pepper

Skin the salmon and check that there are no bones in it, then chop finely. Mix all of the other ingredients with the salmon, seasoning to taste with a little salt and some cayenne pepper.

Serve immediately, with toasted brown bread.

Rosleague chocolate mousse

An inherited speciality, that must be the simplest chocolate mousse ever, this is incredibly easy to make and pleases guests just as much as ever today. As always with very simple dishes, success depends on the quality of ingredients, so it will pay to use the very best quality chocolate you can find.

Serves 4-6
6-8 medium egg whites
8oz / 225g best quality, dark
*   chocolate*

Melt the chocolate in a bowl over a pan of simmering water. Whisk the egg whites until firm. Still using the whisk, combine the chocolate with the egg whites, until they are well mixed, with no flecks of white showing. Pour into a bowl or four individual serving dishes. Place in the fridge and leave overnight before serving. Serve with a teaspoon of whipped cream on top and, perhaps, some seasonal berries.

Stella Maris Hotel

Ballycastle, Co Mayo

Built in 1853 as a coast guard regional headquarters, this fine coastal property on the edge of one of Ireland's most delightful and inspoilt villages was later acquired by the Sisters of Mercy, who named it Stella Maris. It now makes a wonderful small hotel, restored to its original impressive condition, and then some, by proporietors Terence McSweeney and Frances Kelly, who have created a warm and stylish interior, where antiques rub shoulders with contemporary pieces and there's a welcome emphasis on comfort. But the stunning location is this hotel's greatest asset and a conservatory built all along the front takes full advantage of it, allowing guests to relax in comfort and warmth while drinking in the majestic views of the surrounding coastline and sea. Dinner is cooked under Frances' direct supervision and is a very enjoyable experience, based on local ingredients as far as possible, including organic produce from nearby Enniscoe House (see page 84) and also from the hotel's own gardens. Residents have a treat in store each morning, too, as the Stella Maris breakfast is worth lingering over. This is indeed a wonderful retreat.

Warm poached plums

The colour is stunning when served in a white bowl, and it's simple and delicious - no wonder this dessert is a such a success to round off Sunday lunch at Stella Maris. The plums are also great chilled, and served plain for breakfast.

Serves 4
2lb 3oz / 1 kg fresh plums
Syrup:
16fl oz / 450ml / 2 cups water
12fl oz / 350ml / 1²/₃ cups sugar
1 small cinnamon stick
2 slices of orange
Garnish:
sprigs of mint
vanilla ice cream or whipped cream

Using a sharp knife, cut a small cross on the base of each plum. Put the syrup ingredients into a stainless steel saucepan and heat to boiling point. Stir to dissolve the sugar. Add the plums, bring the liquid back to a gentle simmer and cook gently until the plums are softening, but still firm enough to remain whole. Take off the heat and remove the plums from the syrup. Strain the syrup to remove any loose skin particles.

Serve in a shallow bowl, while still warm.

To serve: Put about three or four plums per person and a small ladle of the syrup into individual serving bowls, and serve with vanilla ice cream, or softly whipped cream. Decorate simply with a sprig of fresh mint.

Carrot & orange soup

This soup is very easy to make using ingredients that are readily available in every kitchen. The texture is light, the flavour sweet and refreshing, and the colour presents beautifully in any bowl.

Serves 6

2 oranges
1 large onion, peeled and finely chopped
3 tbsp / 4 US tablespoons sunflower oil or butter
6 carrots, peeled and chopped
1³/₄ pints / 1 litre / 4¹/₂ cups vegetable stock or water
8 fl oz / 225ml / 1 cup orange juice
salt & freshly ground pepper.

Use a citrus zester if you have one, otherwise lightly grate the rind from one orange, being careful to grate only the tangy outer skin and not to grate down to the pith (the white part of the rind). Set aside, then squeeze the juice from both oranges. Measure and make up to 8 fl oz / 225ml / 1 cup with extra juice if necessary. Strain.

In a large saucepan, gently sauté the onion in the sunflower oil or butter for 10 minutes, without colouring. Add the chopped carrots and cook, stirring constantly, for a further 10 minutes, until softening a little. Add the vegetable stock or water and some seasoning, and bring back to the boil. Simmer for 40 minutes or until the carrots are soft. Remove from the heat, add the orange juice and purée in a blender or food processor until smooth, adding more liquid (if necessary) to create a good serving consistency. Check the seasoning and serve hot, garnished with a sprinkling of orange zest.

Tinakilly House

Rathnew, Co Wicklow

Tinakilly was built in the 1870s for Captain Robert Halpin, a local man who made fame and fortune as Commander of The Great Eastern, which laid the first telegraph cable linking Europe and America. Sensitively restored and extended by William and Bee Power, who opened it as an hotel in 1983, it is now owned by their son, Raymond and his wife, Josephine. Professional management with a personal touch, an appealing balance between Victorian charm and modern comfort, and a welcoming fire burning in the lofty entrance hall - plus an excellent location easily accessible to Dublin, yet definitely "in the country" - have combined to make Tinakilly one of Ireland's most successful country house hotels. Good food is vital to the formula, of course - and the kitchen garden produces

an abundance of fruit and vegetables for most of the year and this, plus local produce and seafood, provides the basis for excellent updated country house cooking.

White chocolate & Baileys mousse with raspberries

A fruit farm near Tinakilly House supplies the kitchen with fresh raspberries all through the summer. The combination of white chocolate and Baileys in this simple sweet complements the tartness of the berries perfectly to create a totally delectable dessert.

Serves 4-5

9oz / 250ml / 1 cup plus 2 US tablespoons cream
1¹/₂ fl oz / 40ml / 3 US tablespoons Baileys Irish Cream liqueur
5oz / 150g white chocolate (buttons, or a bar broken into pieces)
8oz / 225g / 2 cups raspberries

Place the cream and the Baileys in a saucepan, bring to a simmer and then remove from the heat.

Place the chocolate in a bowl and pour the heated cream over it. Stir until completely mixed, with no lumps of chocolate remaining. Cover with cling film and allow to cool for about half an hour at room temperature, then place in the fridge for about 2-3 hours to cool completely.

Gently wash the raspberries in cold water and allow to drain on kitchen paper. Beat the fully chilled chocolate mixture in a small mixer, or with an electric hand mixer until it looks like stiffly whipped cream, scraping down the sides of the bowl occasionally.

To serve: Dip a tablespoon in hot water and curl it slowly across the top of the mousse, giving you a quenelle shape (like a rugby ball). For each person place 2 or 3 of these in a bowl, surround with raspberries and serve immediately.

Parcel baked monkfish with tomatoes and basil

This dish keeps to a golden rule of fish cooking, "keep it simple", allowing the flavours to stand out and not be overcrowded. Monkfish is one of the most popular fish available today and this dish is a straightforward approach to what many see as the unnerving experience of fish cookery.

Serves 4

*4 x 5-6 oz / 150-175g portions of
  monkfish tail, trimmed*
1 jar (14oz / 400g) tomato passata
*2oz / 50g / 1 cup basil, roughly
  chopped*
*2oz / 50g / $\frac{1}{2}$ cup red onion, finely
  sliced*
9oz / 250g / 1 cup cherry tomatoes
4 x 8inch / 20cm squares of tinfoil
*4 turns of freshly ground black
  pepper*

Preheat a fairly hot oven, 375°F / 190°C / gas mark 5.

Cut the trimmed monkfish tails in half and place in a large bowl; add the passata, chopped basil and ground black pepper, mixing so that all fillets are well coated in sauce and basil. Place four sheets of tin foil on a flat surface and divide the red onion between them. placing it in the middle of each piece, then lay the fish on top of this. Pull the sides of the foil upwards to make a bowl shape; add the cherry tomatoes and divide the remaining sauce between the four parcels. Bring all the sides of the foil together to close the parcels and squeeze tightly to seal. Be careful not to tear the foil; if it is torn it will need to be re-wrapped. Place the parcels on a baking tray and cook in the preheated oven for 15 minutes. To check if it is cooked, open one parcel and feel if the fish is firm to the touch.

To serve: Open the parcels carefully, as hot steam will escape. Empty each parcel onto a warmed plate or shallow serving bowl, and serve with boiled new potatoes.

Wineport Lodge
Glasson, Athlone, Co Westmeath

The name of Jane English and Ray Byrne's wonderful lakeside restaurant and accommodation is taken from the townland name of its location and, since opening in 1993, it has grown considerably to meet demand as their fame has spread. A stunning location and exceptional hospitality from Ray and Jane and their terrific staff draw guests back time and again - guests who return bearing additions to the now famous Wineport collections (nauticalia, cats) and find the combination of the view, the company and a good meal in this fine restaurant irresistible. Using the best ingredients - including Donald Russell beef, local game in season, eels, home-grown herbs, free range eggs and wild mushrooms - head chef Feargal O'Donnell's strongly seasonal menus are international in style yet, as demonstrated by the recipes below, there is also a definite modern Irish slant. Luxurious accommodation is also offered, in twenty spacious rooms overlooking the lake and designed to take full advantage of the lovely location.

Summer leaf salad with Hick's black pudding, new potatoes and a softly poached egg

The emergence of traditional black pudding as a popular contemporary ingredient is perhaps one of Ireland's more surprising recent culinary developments, and each chef has a favourite supplier. At Wineport this versatile ingredient works well in several dishes, including this tasty warm salad.

Serves 2 as starter or light main course

1 bowl of mixed leaves (oakleaf, rocket, beet leaf, little gem)
4oz / 110g Hick's black pudding, sliced
3 new potatoes, cooked & quartered
A little Cajun spice seasoning (optional)
2 free range eggs, poached
1 bunch watercress

Dressing:
1 tbsp / 1¼ US tablespoons grain mustard
2 tbsp / 2½ US tablespoons aged balsamic vinegar
1 tbsp / 1¼ US tablespoons honey
4 tbsp / 5 US tablespoons vegetable oil
salt and freshly ground pepper

Wash and dry the salad leaves.

In a hot pan brushed lightly with oil, sauté the black pudding and potatoes until the potatoes are nicely browned. Season to taste with Cajun spices, or salt and freshly ground pepper.

Mix all the dressing ingredients together well, to form an emulsion; taste and adjust the seasoning if necessary.

To serve: Poach the eggs in simmering water with a little vinegar added until just cooked; drain well. Toss the salad leaves in the dressing and place in a bowl, or on a serving plate. Arrange the cooked black pudding and potatoes on top, add the soft poached egg and serve immediately.

Mustard crusted rack of lamb, with celeriac dauphinoise

This dish has been a long term success story at Wineport: it is the crust that really brings out and complements the flavour of the lamb. Ask your butcher to prepare the racks by French trimming, i.e.removing the chine bone and cap, and cleaning and trimming the rib bone.

Serves 4
*2 half racks of lamb, French trimmed
    by your butcher (6-8 cutluts on each)*
For the crust:
*5oz / 150g / 1¹/₄ cups dried
    breadcrumbs
2 sprigs each: fresh mint, rosemary &
    parsley
2 cloves garlic
grated rind of 1 lemon
4 tbsp / 5 US tablespoons olive oil
4 tbsp / 5 US tablespoons sweet
    (brown French) mustard*
For the celeriac dauphinoise:
*2 heads celeriac
1 pint / 600ml / 2³/₄ cups cream
2 cloves garlic, crushed
salt and pepper*
Garnish:
*a crunchy green vegetable, and some
    mint jelly*

Preheat a moderate oven, 350°F / 180°C / gas mark 4.

Blend together all the crust ingredients except the mustard. Set aside. Seal the lamb in hot oil and leave to rest.

When ready to cook, brush the lamb liberally with the mustard and coat generously with the herb crust mixture. Cook in the pre-heated oven for about 25 minutes for pink, or about 45 minutes for well done. Allow to rest for 10 minutes before serving.

While the lamb is cooking, peel and roughly chop the celeriac, then cook in boiling water until soft. Drain well, add the cream and crushed garlic, and season well. Boil until the cream thickens, then purée the mixture in a blender until smooth, checking the seasoning at the end.

To serve: Spoon the celeriac mixture onto warm plates and then carve the lamb into cutlets. Serve with some crunchy green vegetables and a little mint jelly.

Ireland

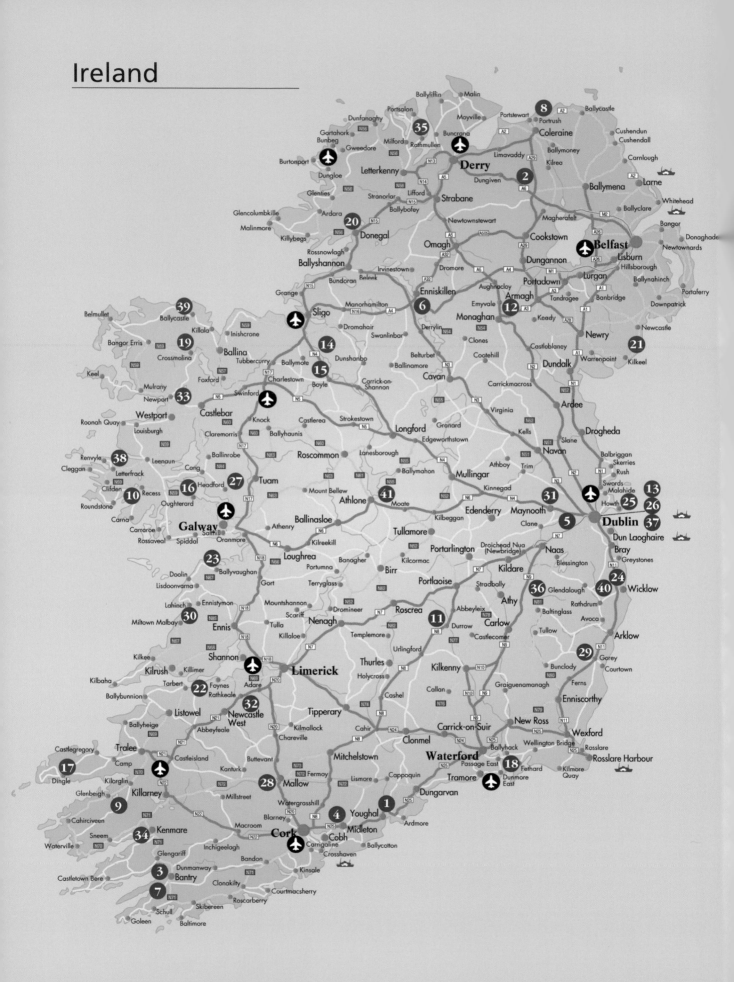

Map References

Each house or restaurant featured in Irish Country House Cooking has a reference number which relates to the map opposite, and recipes in the book are listed in the same order.

1. Aherne's Seafood Bar & Accommodation
   Tel: 024-92424   www.ahernes.com

2. Ardtara Country House
   Tel: +44-28-7964 4490   www.ardtara.com

3. Ballylickey Manor House
   Tel: 027-50071   www.ballylickeymanorhouse.com

4. Ballymaloe House
   Tel: 021-465 2531   www.ballymaloe.ie

5. Barberstown Castle
   Tel: 01-628 8157   www.barberstowncastle.ie

6. Belle Isle Castle
   Tel: +44-28-6638 7231
   www.belleislecastle.com

7. Blairs Cove Restaurant & Accommodation
   Tel: 027-61127

8. Bushmills Inn
   Tel: +44-28-2073 3000   www.bushmillsinn.com

9. Caragh Lodge
   Tel: 066-976 9115   www.caraghlodge.com

10. Cashel House Hotel
    Tel: 095-31001   www.cashel-house-hotel.com

11. Castle Durrow
    Tel: 0502-36555   www.castledurrow.com

12. Castle Leslie
    Tel: 047-88100   www.castleleslie.com

13. Chapter One Restaurant
    Tel: 01-873 2266

14. Coopershill House
    Tel: 071-916 5108   www.coopershill.com

15. Cromleach Lodge
    Tel: 071-916 5155   www.cromleach.com

16. Currarevagh House
    Tel: 091-552312 / 3   www.currarevagh.com

17. Doyle's Seafood Restaurant & Townhouse
    Tel: 066-915 1174   www.doylesofdingle.com

18. Dunbrody House Hotel
    Tel: 051-389600   www.dunbrodyhouse.com

19. Enniscoe House
    Tel: 096-31112   www.enniscoe.com

20. St. Ernan's House Hotell
    Tel: 074-972 1065   www.sainternans.com

21. Glassdrumman Lodge
    Tel: +44-28-437 68451

22. Glin Castle
    Tel: 068-34173   www.glincastle.com

23. Gregans Castle Hotel
    Tel: 065-707 7005   www.gregans.ie

24. Hunter's Hotel
    Tel: 0404-40106   www.hunters.ie

25. King Sitric Fish Restaurant & Accommodation
    Tel: 01-832 5235   www.kingsitric.ie

26. L'Ecrivain Restaurant
    Tel: 01-661 1919   www.lecrivain.com

27. Lisdonagh House
    Tel: 093-31163   www.lisdonagh.com

28. Longueville House
    Tel: 022-47156   www.longuevillehouse.ie

29. Marlfield House
    Tel: 055-21124   www.marlfieldhouse.com

30. Moy House
    Tel: 065-708 2800   www.moyhouse.com

31. Moyglare Manor
    Tel: 01-628 6351   www.moyglaremanor.ie

32. The Mustard Seed at Echo Lodge
    Tel: 069-68508   www.mustardseed.ie

33. Newport House
    Tel: 098-41222   www.newporthouse.ie

34. Park Hotel Kenmare
    Tel: 064-41200   www.parkkenmare.com

35. Rathmullan House
    Tel: 074-915 8188   www.rathmullanhouse.com

36. Rathsallagh House
    Tel: 045-403112   www.rathsallagh.com

37. Restaurant Patrick Guilbaud
    Tel: 01-676 4192
    www.restaurantpatrickguilbaud.ie

38. Rosleague Manor
    Tel: 095-41101   www.rosleague.com

39. Stella Maris Hotel
    Tel: 096-43322   www.StellaMarisIreland.com

40. Tinakilly House Hotel
    Tel: 0404-69274   www.tinakilly.ie

41. Wineport Lodge
    Tel: 0906-439010   www.wineport.ie

Some guests may like to record their visits,
by collecting chefs' signatures in the spaces below.

1. Aherne's Seafood Bar & Accommodation
    Tel: 024-92424   www.ahernes.com

8. Bushmills Inn
    Tel: +44-28-2073 3000   www.bushmillsinn.com

_____

2. Ardtara Country House
    Tel: +44-28-7964 4490   www.ardtara.com

9. Caragh Lodge
    Tel: 066-976 9115   www.caraghlodge.com

_____

3. Ballylickey Manor House
    Tel: 027-50071   www.ballylickeymanorhouse.com

10. Cashel House Hotel
    Tel: 095-31001   www.cashel-house-hotel.com

_____

4. Ballymaloe House
    Tel: 021-465 2531   www.ballymaloe.ie

11. Castle Durrow
    Tel: 0502-36555   www.castledurrow.com

_____

5. Barberstown Castle
    Tel: 01-628 8157   www.barberstowncastle.ie

12. Castle Leslie
    Tel: 047-88100   www.castleleslie.com

_____

6. Belle Isle Castle
    Tel: +44-28-6638 7231
    www.belleislecastle.com

13. Chapter One Restaurant
    Tel: 01-873 2266

_____

7. Blairs Cove Restaurant & Accommodation
    Tel: 027-61127

14. Coopershill House
    Tel: 071-916 5108   www.coopershill.com

_____

15. Cromleach Lodge
    Tel: 071-916 5155   www.cromleach.com

16. Currarevagh House
    Tel: 091-552312 / 3   www.currarevagh.com

17. Doyle's Seafood Restaurant & Townhouse
    Tel: 066-915 1174   www.doylesofdingle.com

18. Dunbrody House Hotel
    Tel: 051-389600   www.dunbrodyhouse.com

19. Enniscoe House
    Tel: 096-31112   www.enniscoe.com

20. St. Ernan's House Hotel
    Tel: 074-972 1065   www.sainternans.com

21. Glassdrumman Lodge
    Tel: +44-28-437 68451

22. Glin Castle
    Tel: 068-34173   www.glincastle.com

23. Gregans Castle Hotel
    Tel: 065-707 7005   www.gregans.ie

24. Hunter's Hotel
    Tel: 0404-40106   www.hunters.ie

25. King Sitric Fish Restaurant & Accommodation
    Tel: 01-832 5235   www.kingsitric.ie

26. L'Ecrivain Restaurant
    Tel: 01-661 1919   www.lecrivain.com

27. Lisdonagh House
    Tel: 093-31163   www.lisdonagh.com

28. Longueville House
    Tel: 022-47156   www.longuevillehouse.ie

29. Marlfield House
Tel: 055-21124   www.marlfieldhouse.com

36. Rathsallagh House
Tel: 045-403112   www.rathsallagh.com

30. Moy House
Tel: 065-708 2800   www.moyhouse.com

37. Restaurant Patrick Guilbaud
Tel: 01-676 4192
www.restaurantpatrickguilbaud.ie

31. Moyglare Manor
Tel: 01-628 6351   www.moyglaremanor.ie

38. Rosleague Manor
Tel: 095-41101   www.rosleague.com

32. The Mustard Seed at Echo Lodge
Tel: 069-68508   www.mustardseed.ie

39. Stella Maris Hotel
Tel: 096-43322   www.StellaMarisIreland.com

33. Newport House
Tel: 098-41222   www.newporthouse.ie

40. Tinakilly House Hotel
Tel: 0404-69274   www.tinakilly.ie

34. Park Hotel Kenmare
Tel: 064-41200   www.parkkenmare.com

41. Wineport Lodge
Tel: 0906-439010   www.wineport.ie

35. Rathmullan House
Tel: 074-915 8188   www.rathmullanhouse.com

Index